The 5 Pillars

of

Accelerated Learning

for

Busy People

64 Practical Techniques to Improve Focus,
Concentration, and Memory. Rapid Knowledge
Acquisition for Academic, Work, and Business Success

◂————●————▸

NEIL KRISTOFF COOPER

Table of Contents

Introduction

If you have picked up this book, it is likely that there are many things that you have wanted to learn in your life—things that have piqued your interest, or could help move you forward in your career, but that you have not yet grasped the knowledge necessary to master those subjects. Regardless of your motivation, these new sets of skills and areas of expertise could help your life; yet the required time and effort have been holding you back from truly making progress when it comes to any of it. There is a way around this—a way that you can make this happen and accomplish what you need to; all you have to do is unlock the secrets of becoming a more effective learner.

In this book, I will share with you 64 accelerated learning hacks that can shape the way that you learn new skills and acquire new knowledge. You will find not only the science behind the theories but also strategies and practical advice that you can readily apply in your daily life, so that you can master new skills with greater speed and efficiency.

Having climbed up the proverbial corporate ladder, I had to continually learn new skills and update my knowledge as I took on new roles and responsibilities. Thanks to the techniques and strategies that I share in this book, I have been able to unleash the power of my mind and train my brain regardless of where I am in my personal or professional life. These strategies were what granted me this ability, improving my life tremendously. And now, through this book, I am sharing what I know with you, hoping that in my heart it will be as helpful for you as it was for me—if not more so!

The contents of this book take on a holistic approach, granting you a backstage pass to the different ways that you can accelerate your learning; from being able to master skills that you are passionate about, to handling pressures that you encounter at work. You will be able to teach yourself how to become a more effective and efficient learner if you read carefully and keep the advice found in this book close to heart.

Each of the first four chapters will take a deeper look into the theories that make up accelerated learning, whereas the chapters that follow will outline the different methodologies, techniques, and systems that you can choose from to equip yourself with this valuable skill. While you can read through the entire book in one sitting, or even skip past the various theories to jump right into the strategies used for learning, I find that knowing why something works is a key step in processing how it works; it gives your mind more pieces of information to grasp onto, similar to having various bits of a jigsaw puzzle completed. For instance, if you do not have even a single piece set down, it can be overwhelming to start filling in the puzzle; however, if you have the corners done already, it gives you important groundwork that you can expand upon until eventually the full picture is completed. Keeping any sort of information in mind is thus much like a jigsaw puzzle; and so, while you are free to read this book in any way you like, I do recommend that you at least keep the theories in mind, even if your main focus is going to be the techniques listed in the later chapters.

The end goal of this book is to help you understand how to accelerate the learning process for yourself so that you can steer your life in the direction that you want, and do it fast, efficiently, and effectively. If at this point in your life, learning feels like it takes ages to get done, I guarantee that the advice contained here will speed that process up so much that you will be shocked at how fast you can process information after using these techniques. Explore various ways to learn quickly while also improving your memory for work and personal success.

You are the only person capable of changing your life. No one can do that for you. If you are up for challenging your brain to seek and perform at a higher level when it comes to obtaining information and skills, the knowledge I am bestowing upon you will help you reach your maximum potential. The strategies you are about to read are proven to yield incredible results for people who want to jumpstart their learning speed abilities. Each chapter in this book will teach you the different theories and techniques that you can implement on your own accelerated learning journey. All you have to do is keep them in mind, practice them yourself, and believe in your ability to learn better than you ever have before.

PILLAR 1:
FOUNDATIONS

Chapter 1:

Things You Wish You Knew About Accelerated Learning

◆·————— ● —————·◆

Accelerated learning is a term that has been thrown around a lot in the post-pandemic zeitgeist, as many people are still struggling to regain the time that they lost during the strongest waves of the virus. As such, the idea of being able to speed up the way you learn while still obtaining all the necessary information you would have obtained during "regular" education is quite an alluring one. However, the term has been used improperly by many groups, since it can be a bit of a buzzword—anything that sounds like faster learning might, therefore, also sound like it is accelerated learning.

Of course, all of this asks a bigger question: Is it even worth worrying about what actually accelerated learning is? Is it something that is worth your time at all, or is it just another new trend to be jumped on and then forgotten after a few months? All these dynamics and more will be explained in time, as I help you understand things that many wish they had known about accelerated learning before.

What It Is (And What It Is Not)

If you want to be able to properly retain the information that you get through educating yourself quickly, then you must understand what accelerated learning is, and what it is not. To put it briefly; accelerated learning is deeper learning that prioritizes higher-level skills and crucial knowledge, trimming the "fat" of a topic to only focus on the relevant parts. All of this can be achieved through creating plans about the information and learning, following through by setting education goals, and properly unlocking what you need to while trying to avoid the irrelevant points related to a topic.

The most common misconceptions about accelerated learning are ones that take that first word, accelerated, perhaps a bit too seriously. Yes, accelerated learning techniques indeed allow you to learn faster; however, trying to simply rush through things is how you end up learning absolutely nothing at all. It could be said that this is decelerated learning, even! Typically, an issue that comes up when someone attempts to take part in accelerated learning without actually knowing what it is tends to be the lack of a "priority queue"; in a sense, you need to keep in mind what to prioritize and what to cut away, rather than trying to absorb everything and hoping that the important bits stick with you.

In trying to describe the difference between these two approaches in a single word, "strategy" would be the best one; rushing recklessly into self-education is the quickest way to give yourself bad information, while taking it slowly at first will allow you to speed ahead at surprising rates. The best comparison would be using an ax to cut down a tree: If you attempt to cut down a tree with an unsharpened ax, it would take four hours to do so—much like trying to rush in without applying accelerated learning. However, if you spend an hour sharpening that ax—making a strategy for how to tackle your learning—then it would only take an hour to cut down that tree, taking you two hours total.

To move fast through the whole process, you have to take it slow at the very beginning; it might seem counter-intuitive but using an acceleration strategy is the most efficient way to go forwards with accelerated learning, rather than trying to do everything on the fly.

The Purpose Behind Using Accelerated Learning (And the Benefits)

Now that you know the general distinction between what makes something accelerated learning, and what is just an attempt at rushing your learning, a question naturally comes to mind: Why even care about it? This is a very logical question to ask, and something that has been asked many times—and while an answer to that question might not necessarily satisfy everyone who asks it, the most common answer relates to the nature of purposeful education; in other words, asking yourself what your purpose is behind learning whatever it is that you're trying to learn?

There are many principles of accelerated learning, but the most relevant one to delve into at this point relates to the nature of knowledge—which was put best by The Peak Performance Center as "the principle that knowledge is not something which the learner absorbs, but something that a learner creates" ("Accelerated Learning", 2022).

In other words, you can only find information that is relevant to what you want if you really want it; however, this could be seen as an aspect of confirmation bias, but that is a gross misinterpretation of the concepts present for accelerated learning. It is not that you are ignoring what you do not want to find, but rather, you need to be willing to accept the information for what it is and actively seek it out in whatever way stimulates and interests you the most. Therefore, it is actually the exact opposite of confirmation bias, and thus trying to go about accelerated learning without this principle in mind may lead you to, indeed, engage in confirmation bias—something that you absolutely want to avoid when it comes to educating yourself.

Now with that purpose in mind, we come to the important question of whether it even works—and the best way to answer this is by explaining how it works, rather than just claiming that it does. The brain is a complicated thing, but the most important brain function to take note of for this book, is the fact that parallel processes in the mind tend to work better than doing things sequentially. Therefore, by using accelerated learning to stimulate multiple senses at the same time and incorporating that into your acceleration strategies, you can use all of those senses to learn what is most important for you at the moment.

This outlook on the brain and how it relates to accelerated learning is reflected by the critical theory perspective; research by Stephen Brookfield of Antioch University corroborates these ideas, stating that from an educational standpoint, courses that use accelerated learning's strategies, "further develop study skills because they require independent study" (Brookfield, 2003, p. 74), allows an individual who engages with it to improve in learning across the board. After all, improving your ability to learn, naturally, allows you to understand more skills and techniques in a snowball-like effect of education. The study conducted by Brookfield primarily relates to how accelerated learning affects school education—and while that is where a lot of the research regarding accelerated learning tends to be focused, the key concepts can also easily apply to individuals who want to improve their own learning, outside of a school setting.

Little-Known Dynamics of Accelerated Learning

In any sort of change in perspective, it is important to understand the dynamics of the change, so that it can be properly used. However, while accelerated learning in relation to public education is well-documented and reported on, there is little work that truly dives deeply into the topic of how it relates to individual adults. Learning, contrary to what some might say, is not something that stops at any point in our lives; from adolescence to adulthood, we are still picking up new skills, and so neglecting that in favor of exclusively focusing on the educational system is a bit disingenuous.

Therefore, while it is important for educators and parents to understand the dynamics of accelerated learning for their students and children, it is also important to dig deeper and comprehend these dynamics for personal education as well.

One of the most integral (and yet often overlooked) dynamics to be found when it comes to accelerated learning is the relationship between the learner and what they are learning; while it can be summed up in a variety of ways, the easiest way to put it is that the learner is at the "center" of a redefined educational experience. You could describe a typical learning method as being almost like a two-dimensional plane, where the person learning is moving across a flat path; they do make progress, but in a very linear fashion, picking up information in a "standard" order. In comparison, accelerated learning is more like placing yourself (the learner) in the center of a three-dimensional space filled with knowledge, and moving toward the most relevant information at a much faster rate. While it is true that learning in this fashion is not something that will appeal to everyone, and some truly do thrive best in that more linear format, studies on accelerated learning have found that around 42% of adults tend towards using non-traditional learning methods, finding great success with accelerated learning techniques compared to the more traditional styles of education (Marques, 2012).

Another important dynamic to keep in mind is the way that accelerated learning compares to regular learning in terms of its structure—or, in other words, dispelling the misconception that it is just "regular learning, but faster". While this book has already gone over the exact details in terms of speed, what is more, relevant here is clarification on the nature of how responsibility factors in. When it comes to accelerated learning, there is significantly more responsibility being placed on the learner's shoulders; compared to a more traditional format with a teacher, where it becomes a mutual sort of responsibility between the educator and their student. Either way, self-education or not, if you are to use accelerated learning techniques, you are responsible for designing your education in a way that will both suit your needs and heighten the speed at which you do things. It was put best by Swenson (2003, p. 84), who stated that "A learner's preferred learning style, dominant perceptual mode, role, motivation, interest in the subject matter, and other variables combine to make every individual learning transaction a universe of one".

Ironically, if you want to use accelerated learning to its fullest potential, you also need to understand bits and pieces about the topic that you are trying to educate yourself on. This, among other reasons, is a defining factor for why conversations about accelerated learning tend to include the assumption that it is for adolescent education, rather than self-education; however, dismissing the idea of using it for self-education is missing out on the great potential that it grants. Provided that the learner is highly motivated, willing to go the extra mile to make sure that they properly understand what they are getting into, and can put in the extra effort to make use of accelerated learning techniques, it truly is a method that can help many adults find so much success.

Before closing off this section, we need to address the fact that there is a dynamic that is a negative for accelerated learning; clarity—or, more accurately, a lack thereof. When it comes to changing the ways that you learn things, there is a natural resistance to newer methods, and it can be unclear how to begin; accelerated learning, much like any other alternative learning technique, is no different. It can be challenging to write a comprehensive guide to direct an individual on how best to handle this because it really is a world in itself for each person—mastering accelerated learning requires a deep understanding of your own preferences for processing information, finding out the strategies that will work for you to digest what you come across, and preparing yourself for some amounts of trial and error.

In the next chapter, we will go over various principles related to accelerated learning, which should be kept in mind as potential guidelines for finding out what works best for you—much like sharpening an axe, there are many ways to go about it, and not every principle will be of preference for you. Provided you use some critical thinking skills to properly judge which principles are the most fitting for your learning style, you should be able to apply accelerated learning to your future self-education endeavors.

PILLAR 2:
PRINCIPLES

Chapter 2:

7 Principles of Accelerated Learning

While there are a variety of ways to outline the tenets of accelerated learning, they can be summed up overall through 7 main principles: multi-sensory learning, visual aspects of learning, the learner's emotions, the learning environment, creative aspects related to education, feedback, and collaboration. The nuances of these principles are what truly define accelerated learning, and play a key part in understanding an individual's learning style—an immensely important step to actually using accelerated learning for yourself.

Multi-Sensory Learning

Essentially, multi-sensory learning is the concept that education is something that requires your entire body; yes, learning indeed involves your brain, but it is not exclusively tied to that part of you to the point that you can just ignore everything else. Other receptors that affect your mental state and ability to process new information must be kept in mind and wielded as a tool to properly make use of accelerated learning.

For instance, imagine that you grew up in a house where apple pies were frequently baked; as a result, you would likely associate the smell of apple pies with ideas of home. This same sort of connection can be applied to information as well—if you associate a piece of knowledge with some form of sensory experience, then when that sense is reactivated, your memories of that knowledge can also be accessed. Some people use flavors of chewing gum, for instance, as a way to "unlock" their memories by chewing a certain kind of gum when studying for a subject, and having that same flavor when they need to recall it (such as during an exam). While taste is just one of the many senses that could be used for a technique such as this—and really, taste *alone* is not usually good enough when trying to understand an entire subject—it is certainly an effective sense to use, especially due to the easy access of a variety of edible things.

However, the senses are just a single part of multi-sensory learning; while speaking more of the *body* in how it relates to learning, there is also the rest of the mind itself.

Visual Learning

As using the brain is how we can learn anything at all, understanding how it functions and what it absorbs best is integral for any kind of learning strategy—both alternative tactics, and more traditional ones as well. In the case of accelerated learning, one piece of information above many others is critical to keep in mind: How the brain processes visual stimuli. When it comes to efficiency, visual information is the absolute fastest way for the brain to retain and recall relative amounts of detail; an image that is much more concrete and defined can be remembered with surprising accuracy, compared to many other sensory methods. Of course, neglecting your other senses would not be a good idea, but focusing on visuals is an extremely effective method for many.

The best way to think of it is almost like a program on a computer; Google Docs is excellent for handling text, but it can sometimes struggle to handle images—Photoshop, on the other hand, is perfect for editing visual information, but when it comes to large chunks of text, such as essays, it would be much easier to format it in another program like Google Docs. When thinking about the brain, it could be compared to Photoshop more than Google Docs; for the brain, processing images is much easier than processing text. Certainly, you can create many things using text in Photoshop, and in fact, you most likely need to for the majority of projects that use it—but images are where the program shines, being the simplest and most efficient use of what you have available.

With this in mind, when trying to apply visual techniques to accelerated learning, you need to discover ways to translate more "normal" types of information (such as text or voice recordings) into visuals; graphs and flowcharts are two common methods, making use of a variety of colors, shapes, and connections to try and piece together the whole picture. For instance, if you need to distinguish between four different sections of information, you might make a graph that contains four distinct images in a two-by-two grid, with a triangle in the top left, a circle in the bottom left, a square in the top right, and an oval in the bottom right. By associating these shapes with the information that you need, you can quickly sketch this image grid on an exam you are taking—or whatever other piece of paper you might have nearby—and thus bring it back into the focus of your mind within a few moments. If this specific strategy does not work for you, all you need to do is examine what you have at hand in terms of data, and then process it into a different kind of graph; for many, this is one of the most effective and practical strategies for retaining larger amounts of information.

Emotional Learning

At a glance, it might sound as if emotions should not be thought of when considering something as "logical" as learning; however, a person's emotional state can actually contribute a lot when it comes to processing information. Studies conducted by the Peak Performance Center have determined that positive emotions and excitement make it easier for us to retain the information; on the other hand, if you are stressed out, bored, or otherwise consumed by melancholy, then it is much harder to remember what you are being told ("Accelerated Learning", 2022).

Think of it in another way; imagine something about one of your hobbies, you can recall many specific details about it, can you not? You might be able to easily list off the rules of your favorite card game, know some precise terminology for how to place chess pieces on a board, or recall the exact numbers used for aspects of your most preferred sport—all this information could come without a struggle if you have delved deep into your hobbies, and done your best to learn about them. Yet, if you try to do the same with something academic, or even with a new hobby that you are not "clicking" with even though you desperately want to, it is significantly more challenging.

While not the only explanation, a very likely one is the fact that when it comes to those less "fun" topics, you have not been feeling positive emotions when it came to educating yourself on them. Perhaps you wanted to paint, but any time you picked up the brush and started to replicate the shape of an apple, you noticed that your brushstrokes were always going too far, or it made what should have been an almost geometric shape appear to be more like something out of a horror film's special effects for gore? If you beat yourself up about the learning process, you will actually make it harder for yourself to learn; and if that applies to you, then you need to do your best to accept the process for what it is, and rather than berate yourself, do your best to make it into something fun.

Lastly on the topic of emotions, while emotions in the truest sense— as in, distinct feelings that you, well, *feel*—are the most notable part of this principle, personal motivation should also be considered. To put it in other words: Do you have a strong reason that motivates you to take your learning seriously? If your only motivation for learning something is "just to learn it" or "for fun and nothing else" you may have some struggles with your ability to properly take part in accelerated learning; of course, due to the way that everyone's emotional states are different, reasons such as those could work just fine! However, if at all possible, it is recommended that you try to motivate yourself in a way that your mind would see as more "serious" in some fashion. For instance, if you have always wanted to complete some dream project, but lacked the skills to do so; well, what you are learning right now can be seen as just another step towards achieving that dream!

Your Learning Environment

Where you learn is arguably just as important as the strategies you employ in the learning itself; for instance, if you are trying to educate yourself in the same room that you eat in, you might either associate learning too much with eating (and thus could easily get distracted) or the other way around (and thus make eating stressful during any period where the self-education process is getting rough). Yet, it also does not inherently mean you should go to some dull office space where all of the life is sucked out of you—as we just went over, your emotional state is important for your ability to use accelerated learning techniques (or, really, *any* kind of learning at all). So, if you are in an environment that makes you feel so much nothing that you might as well become a black hole, then it is *also* a bad environment for education.

When it comes to picking out the proper learning environment, you should be willing to experiment; rather than just think of one room and commit to it, try out a variety of different locations around your house, community, or anywhere else that would work best for you—and take notes on the effects that each environment has had on you! If there are places where you feel like you have a relaxed emotional state, you feel a strong sense of discipline to keep working on your education, and there are no readily available distractions to take your focus away; well, in that case, you have likely found an excellent spot for you to learn in.

To go further, however, you can attempt to create an accelerated learning environment—a space that is specifically catered to accelerated learning. First and foremost, you need it to be a positive learning environment, just like discussed above; after you have acquired such a space, you need to make sure that it is positive in three aspects: physical, emotional, and social. These, as defined by the Peak Performance Center ("Accelerated Learning", 2022), can be boiled down to the room being comfortable, having enough bright light—ideally, with windows—as well as colors, and overall having a relaxed feeling to it all. The social aspect can be difficult if you are participating in self-education, but it can be supplemented through taking occasional breaks while having your learning environment near where you could interact with someone for a short while—such as by texting on your phone or being near a park.

Ultimately, what will work best for your learning environment will depend on your individual preferences. The best advice I can give is for you to experiment a bit; even if something works all right, try to see if you can push it further. If you keep trying, you might just find something which can help you learn even better.

Creation in Education

One of the most important principles of accelerated learning is the idea that information is not just something you absorb but rather, it is something that you help create as you learn. Now, this does not mean that you are just imagining something out of thin air when it comes to learning about a topic; rather, it means that you are creating new pathways for the knowledge that you find, allowing yourself to incorporate it into your skillset in a more natural, dynamic fashion.

The best way to think of it is almost like connecting highways; at first, you might have two different roads that are going parallel to each other, and lead off in different directions, going to different places—maybe one of them goes to a nice restaurant, while another leads to a theme park. While the roads remain separated, you have to commit to going to one or the other—there is no bridge between them. However, through creating connections with the knowledge you acquire by creating as you learn, it is like you are constructing a connecting highway between these roads, giving you more options with your time.

In trying to integrate creation into how you learn, experimentation is one possible method you can try; applying the skills you already have to the topic you are learning more about is an effective method of experimentation, and—depending on your skillset—it can have very positive returns! Of course, this is not advocating for you to ignore learning any new skills as part of the process, but if you remember how you were able to pick up one such creative hobby (such as writing), you could very likely apply some of those tricks to learning another (such as painting). When it comes to experimentation, you should make sure to keep it relatively light-hearted; hopefully, it will end up making the process of learning much smoother, creating new knowledge that is far easier for you to understand compared to the baseline content—even if it does not, there is no shame in that, and so you should not beat yourself up for a failed experiment. Failure is simply part of the learning process and making yourself feel bad every time you fail is the quickest way to stop learning completely.

In a way, you could look at the discovery of new knowledge as an almost "playful" activity—it can be like a game, where you just try to uncover knowledge and have fun with it all. Stressing out over learning will only serve to make it harder, but trying to enjoy yourself during the process, and create fun ways to engage with the information, will let it stick in your mind with greater strength than just treating it like another bland piece of dull knowledge. Whichever way you end up using creativity to engage with your learning, know that if it is making the process easier or more enjoyable, then it has not been a waste of time and effort; it is just another step on the path to accelerated learning so that you can conquer even the hardest of challenges with efficiency and quality.

Feedback, From Peers and Yourself

In any form of learning, it is naturally important to have some kind of feedback—because if you do not engage in any kind of feedback, how are you to properly know if you are learning or not? There are a variety of ways to engage in feedback, but one of the most common is to have peers who are learning the same things as you are, or who are otherwise more educated in the subject. If you can get such people to help you—either by being friends already or by heading to a place where well-learned individuals of your respective subject reside—it can speed up the rate at which you can learn new skills exponentially.

If these resources are not available to you, however, do not fret—human beings can learn best when there is a level of context to what they are doing, and so you can engage in feedback loops with just yourself. These can broadly be classified into two kinds of self-feedback: suggestion, and de-suggestion. Both of these processes can also be applied when having peers, of course—but for the purpose of describing them, I will assume they are used for self-feedback; know that your mileage may vary, but that they can still function excellently as forms of peer feedback.

Suggestion could be seen as similar to "positive feedback"; for instance, looking at a drawing you did yesterday and one that you did today while taking note of what made the piece you did today look better than the earlier one. You might tell yourself that the way you handled the shading showed a clear improvement and that it really brings out the contours of the shapes you are working with; of course, exact terminology might be difficult to grasp when you are earlier on in a subject. Still, by analyzing your own work and taking note of where you excelled, you can help push yourself forwards to keep learning. Suggestion can also, as the name would suggest, include giving yourself suggestions on how you could improve—yes, that shading was nice, but perhaps instead of using black paint for it, perhaps you could try a shade of blue instead?

De-suggestion, on the other hand, is the exact opposite; you take note of what it is that you were doing incorrectly and tell yourself to avoid doing that. Keep in mind that although this could be framed in a negative light—"you should not have had the main character say their entire backstory on one page, you are an absolute fool and should stop writing"—you should ideally avoid doing something like this. Negative reinforcement like that tends to actually prevent you from properly learning because it stresses you out and makes you want to avoid engaging with the subject. Instead, think of it more as a gentle push toward the direction you want to take yourself in; you were not a moron for having a character use a high amount of exposition, but it would be better if you toned down the level of monologues you went for in your latest short story.

Overall, without feedback it can be difficult to learn properly since you have no real expectations for what you are doing; therefore, either from yourself or from others, you should try to use some form of feedback as a guiding hand on your path to learning. Experiment with various ways to engage with feedback for the best possible results; for instance, perhaps instead of de-suggestion, you focus entirely on suggestion and just keep in mind what you might be doing wrong mentally. It depends significantly on the person which tactics will work the best but provided you try out many different ways to tackle the issue, you will certainly come to find one that works best for you.

Collaborative Learning

Finally, to extrapolate a bit more on what was touched on in the last section, collaborating with others has been shown to increase the effectiveness of learning; having a solid sort of social "base" to jump off from increases the average person's ability to digest information. Typically, it can be seen as similar to how humans tend to be good at remembering faces or recalling details about other people; you might not always be able to say what you like or dislike about someone exactly, but those feelings still exist, and you can paint your mind in vague directions which guide you towards the right answer—maybe it is one of their personality traits or the way that they laugh, or perhaps it is just the fact that you have a common interest? Regardless of the reason, most people can get that far just off of the fact they have interacted with another person.

Thus, learning can work in the same way—it could possibly even be compared to how you might remember a fun vacation with friends more than one you took on your own. Interacting with others in a positive, stress-free way while you educate yourself is part of why schools tend to pair up their students for assignments because collaborative learning is much more effective than solo learning. Of course, keep that part in mind—*collaborative* learning;

it is true that, when engaging in education alongside others, you *could* partake in a sort of competition, trying to "learn the most", "understand the fastest", or something along those lines. For some people, that might seem like the best option and to be honest, if it sounds like it would be the best for you, then it is not a bad idea to at least give it a try.

However, on average, studies performed by groups such as the Peak Performance Center have shown that competition actually tends to disparage the topic that the participants are learning, and instead, make them focus much more on beating the other people in the contest ("Accelerated Learning", 2022). As a result, most individuals do not actually retain the knowledge that they are learning, because their minds are preoccupied with thinking about how it is that they are going to win, how they did win, how they lost, and so on. In comparison, collaborative learning makes it much more of a team effort, and so everyone is occupied with trying to tackle the problems of understanding what they are doing—this process that we all know as "learning".

Applying the Principles

When it comes to the principles that have been outlined in this chapter, keep in mind that nothing here is an ironclad rule; you should try to follow them when starting, of course, but as I have done my best to stress, *experimentation is key*; some of these techniques will work better for you than others, and if you just follow them to the letter simply due to the fact I have said to, then that would hurt your ability to learn. Instead, it is recommended that you use these "rules" more like guidelines; follow them where they sound best, but if you have tried out new ideas and they worked better, or you found that some of the suggestions given here ended up hurting your learning process, then feel free to do things your own way! At the end of the day, there is more than one way to do most things, and accelerated learning is no exception.

PILLAR 3:
CHARACTERISTICS

Chapter 3:

13 Characteristics of Accelerated Learning You Should Know

◆———•———◆

Now that you understand how to engage with accelerated learning more, you might be asking yourself: Is keeping all of this in mind even worth it? Do the benefits of using all of these techniques actually exist, or are they more like placebos planted in the minds of those who do not dig deeper? These are very legitimate concerns to be faced when consulting any sort of self-help book like this one—but in this chapter, allow me to dissuade those fears by giving a deeper dive into the various characteristics of accelerated learning, including examples. After reading this chapter, I guarantee that you will be able to properly "get it" as to why people engage with accelerated learning.

For ease of access, this chapter splits up important characteristics into 13 bullets, listed in bold, followed by a descriptive explanation. I hope that this will assist you if you have been struggling to grasp any of the concepts in here; but of course, feel free to ignore these bits if they are unnecessary for your own memory.

The Benefits Make Sense to Our Human Bodies

1. It focuses on the whole brain. Have you ever heard the myth that we only use ten percent of our brains? It is a very common misconception that has been spread by many—but there is *some* credence to it, in the sense that many aspects of learning do not make use of the entirety of the human mind. When it comes to accelerated learning, the other parts of the brain are used, which allows more retention of knowledge and superior understanding compared to a more narrow-minded approach. In a sense, you can almost think of it like working out; other ways of educating yourself might be like only training a single part of your body—in the short term, it *will* help you make that part of you stronger, but it can be bad for your health to *only* exercise your legs, or your arms, or some other part of you. In comparison, stimulating all of your mind through accelerated learning is a more proper workout that improves your entire body, allowing your newfound strength to be channeled in a much healthier fashion.

2. It is both physical and emotional. Just like a workout, accelerated learning can be much more "physical"; despite what the public education system appears to think, the mind is not the only part of the body that is involved when it comes to comprehending information, and neglecting the rest of your physical needs leads to your brain struggling to understand what it is trying to grasp. Our emotions, too, get involved, and by using them we can recall things with much more ease; people have an easier time bringing up information that they learned through emotions and interactions, compared to those based on a textbook. It is much easier to remember pieces of information about characters in a story you like, or the people you know, compared to what was on page 230 of your science textbook in your 11th-grade science course. Therefore, by involving those emotions in the learning process, you can make use of the brain's superior emotional memory for the benefit of your more academic learning needs.

3. It is both fun and joyful. Lastly, a closing remark related to the body; accelerated learning is also a process that can be filled with much more joy and fun—which are just natural extensions of trying to tie your emotions and physical form into the learning process. If you are happy and enjoying yourself, then you will be able to recall the information that you learn much easier compared to if you are bored and stressed. Education is not a part of life that should be made out to be as awful as other learning techniques have shown it to be, it can be a social experience, one that a person should look forward to, and strive to do their absolute best in.

It Can Be Collaborative

4. It uses collaboration as a medium for understanding. Rather than just have *one* person do their best in learning, why not have multiple people do the same? As examined by Learning Doorway ("Accelerated Learning Principles", 2009), using collaboration when it comes to your learning heightens the ability a person has to understand the information that they are presented with—not just because they have other people who they can "lean on" if they are struggling, but also the fact that it allows an individual to act more like a mentor. While it may sound ironic, trying to teach someone else something can actually give you a greater understanding of what you are teaching; you have to understand the subject well enough to make sure that you are giving accurate advice, and thus your mind is able to focus itself in very different ways compared to more "personal" education.

5. It is holistic and multi-dimensional. Another reason why collaboration is useful for accelerated learning is the fact that it highlights one of the more useful traits of this kind of learning: It can be multi-dimensional. To put it in another way, when it comes to accelerated learning, you can pick up on a variety of skills from just a single source, compared to only mastering one; collaboration heightens this since interacting with other people naturally means you have to use a variety of social skills, while also being able to make use of the knowledge that you are picking up. Thus, your interpersonal skills, your ability to manage time, and other social skills that would be relevant for the specific group you are studying with can be honed by the whetstone of accelerated learning. Of course, this means that picking the group that you are partaking in your learning with is arguably just as important as choosing the subject you are going to be working on together—you want to make sure that they are people that have the kind of experience and insights which would be beneficial for improving your overall educational environment.

6. It can be dynamic. While it is true that working with others is not the ideal solution for *everyone*, for those who feel that they can learn at an acceptable rate when learning alongside others, collaboration is truly one of the strongest benefits of accelerated learning. If you feel that you struggle with social learning, it may be worth at least giving it a try—you might be surprised how useful having other people to learn with can further expedite the learning process.

Accelerated Learning Can Be Results-Based

7. It can fit your needs in a results-based fashion. On the topic of achieving said results, another important characteristic of accelerated learning that you should keep in mind is that it can be particularly results-based. Now, it does not necessarily *have* to be if you are just trying to educate yourself for the sake of education—but for most people who would want to speed up their learning, there is likely something you want to *apply* that knowledge to. Accelerated learning just cannot be beat when it comes to results: You manage to squeeze in far more learning than you would expect you could, in a much shorter amount of time than any sort of other curricula, and typically most people tend to have a greater understanding of the knowledge they acquired than if they had stretched it out over a more typical time period.

8. You are able to learn through activities. Though results are important, something that is equally vital is the way in which those results are achieved; for accelerated learning, this understanding can be obtained through more "activity"-style actions rather than "study"-based ones. In general, a person can use more physical tricks for accelerated learning, making use of actual literal space rather than just intellectual, *metaphorical* space—kinesthetic learning is one term used to refer to this style. In simple terms, it can be thought of as the difference between learning 2 + 2, and someone having two apples, then receiving two more; of course, both of these are understandable to us due to being *extremely* simple, but the same concept applies.

9. Even with more complicated subjects, it can feel natural. As a more complex example, when it comes to how computers comprehend frames through frame rules, it is certainly possible to describe it in more literal terms, relating to how the device's information processor is only able to update at certain frequencies of time, based on algorithms chosen in the code, which is based on which programming language the script was written in for the overall functions of the product. Alternatively, it could be described as a bus, which has a very tight schedule; it arrives once every few minutes, and so you have to either get on at that very moment, or you have to wait a few minutes for your next chance to get on. It is much simpler to understand that way, is it not? The specifics are something that should be learned eventually if you need to delve deeper into comprehending the nature of computer programming—but having a more "physical" image of everything makes it much easier to pick up. This same concept can be applied to any kind of learning, and it is something that accelerated learning particularly favors since its techniques are all finely honed toward learning what is most necessary for you to jump into a deeper understanding of the topic that you are focused on at the moment.

10. It is learner centered. It is this learner-centered aspect of accelerated learning which makes it superior for the people of our modern world to use: It fits into our current societal climate much more snugly than traditional learning strategies. A person's ability to learn in school often has nothing to do with how intelligent they are, but instead how they can process information; of course, there is nothing wrong with these systems when it comes to the people that it works best for—but it should not be seen as the *only* way to understand topics. When it comes to how an individual learns, there are many nuances that need to be understood for the right steps to be taken—steps that traditional learning will not let you take, but you can most certainly do so with accelerated learning.

11. Accelerated learning can nurture creativity. In the world that we live in, you have to not only comprehend various subjects but be able to mash them together with hundreds if not thousands of other topics, trying to create the next big thing. Even if you just want to do something as a hobby, there can always be a strong desire to *make something*; it is true that you could just try to learn a subject and *only* that one subject, without any idea of how it connects to others. However, instead of doing that (as traditional learning would have you do), why not keep the option of intermingling knowledge open?

12. It makes use of all of your senses. As shown in more detail in the previous chapter, all your senses can be stimulated through devising particular strategies for your individual needs, making use of the natural balance between your different senses to enable your mind to retain information with greater detail than you otherwise would. In the interest of not retreading existing ground, chapter 2 gives more of an overview of this topic, while chapter 5 delves deeper if the subject is of particular interest to you.

13. Flexibility can be your focus. Last and certainly not least, you are able to pick and choose which parts of the learning process work best for you and your schedule—regardless of how busy you may be—and all in all, you can still find time to learn what you need to.

PILLAR 4:
PROCESS

Chapter 4:

How to Practice Accelerated Learning in 5 Simple Steps

•————————●————————•

Through everything that you have been reading so far, you must certainly be ready to begin on your journey of improving your ability to learn. Well, a book like this would be lacking in terms of use if it only explained *what* accelerated learning was and left at it that; in this chapter, you will find five simple steps that I have found to be the most effective to follow when it comes to practicing accelerated learning. While these are not even close to the *only* steps one could take to practice accelerated learning—and they will not be the only guides given in this book, of course—they are a very solid framework on which many other techniques are built upon.

The First Step: Preparation

Something that I have done my best to stress over and over in the chapters of this book so far is the fact that you, the person reading this right now, will have to essentially take the role of your own instructor; it is not that you will have to already know everything you want to learn, of course, as that would be impossible and defeat the purpose of learning. No, rather it is the fact that you need to examine what you are learning and make a plan of action for how you will tackle it; in a sense, you can *almost* think of it like the sorts of assignments you would have received in school, except catered to your specific educational needs.

This can be easier if you have already dipped your toes a bit into the topic at hand; if you have already identified some of your struggles—perhaps you struggle to properly draw a straight line when trying to learn more about pencil drawing —then you can make a work plan that lets you locate strategies to improve your weaknesses. If you have not yet done any diving into the topic, that is still fine; just make sure that you do your best to examine the *entirety* of the topic in a relatively quick fashion, pick out the parts that are most relevant to what you need to learn, and then construct a path forward that will let you tackle it.

Preparation is not just limited to a work plan; it can also be based on your mentality. Researchers at classpert.com found that an almost meditation-like personal ritual can work wonders for your focus when it comes to engaging in *any* kind of learning—and especially so for accelerated learning, due to that level of focus giving great-er dividends because of the higher speed of this style (Bernardes, 2019). One such way you can engage in this kind of ritual is by closing your eyes, taking a deep breath, and doing your best to picture what it is that you are going to learn about. There is no need to stress over it—but trying to focus on a plan for how you will tackle it can be quite effective for your mental state. Push away whatever distractions you have that would prevent you from finishing the task at hand, and when you have come back to reality, you can break down the goals that you are trying to strive towards into smaller, more realistic portions. Not to say that you cannot "shoot for the stars" or that you have to downsize your dreams, but more that you have to take tiny steps towards what you want to achieve. Of course, you can *try* to take larger steps instead, but that usually tends to give a higher chance of failure and create false expectations—accelerated learning makes the process of learning *faster*, yet it is not some kind of miracle technique that will make all of your desires happen at the snap of your fingers.

Generally, you can sum up this step as the following: Examine what you are trying to accomplish, take some time to think about it carefully, and make a plan with that knowledge—all of which naturally leads to the next step!

The Second Step: Connection

At the start of this step, you should have some kind of battle plan in motion, and be ready to accomplish your goals; however, in this step, you now have to answer that burning question: What *are* your goals, really? Not in a broader, lifetime goals sort of sense, but the goals for this session of learning; if you were to study for an hour that day as your plan, what would be a successful outcome after that hour? Your expectations must be tempered, realistic, and properly oriented to the roots of the topic that you are going to learn about; you should not expect to master learning fluent Japanese in one day after never having known a single word of it in your life.

As the name implies, this step is about the idea of "connection". When it comes to accelerated learning processes, one of the most important ways to increase the rate at which you can learn is by linking together what you already know with what you are trying to find out more about—and this step is where that comes up! For instance, if you are trying to learn how to play a new instrument, think about what skills you have in life that could apply here; your ability to tackle problems in creative ways, your music tastes, and how easily you might be able to identify notes and pitches, or your skills in a different creative skill. You need to examine your own abilities to get proper answers, and it may take some thinking to see how they could properly align, but it is by using this level of connection that many topics can be understood in a flash.

Another way that this step relates to the concept of connecting is in how what you are learning will impact your life; you must ask yourself: How important is the subject that I am learning? It does not have to be important on a global scale; but, instead, it has to be integral to you on a *personal* level; this could be that it is a skill that would help you get a higher-paying job than the one you have right now, it could be a language that you are learning for the sake of getting closer to a new group of people, or it could even be a niche strategy in one of your favorite games that you are trying to comprehend. Provided that there is something you can latch onto and see as relevant, and that will allow you to take on newer concepts head-on with much greater fervor than if you just went through with it all without caring a little about the subject at hand.

Yet not every topic that you *need* to learn will necessarily seem relevant to you at a glance—and that is both fine and natural! However, if a subject feels like a brick wall that you just need to bash your head through, then you may need to start asking yourself some questions.

Expert economist Felipe Bernardes recommends that you write down your queries based on your initial expectations of the subject and how learning it will be, and as you engage with the topic, you begin to look around for the answers, writing down each one that you find as you locate it. This process is almost like a game in a way: Your mind is engaged, looking for the solutions to the questions that you have posed, and so it tends to be more receptive to the information that is being provided to it during this activity.

In short, this step can be summed up as making sure that the topic is relevant and engaging to you in some fashion; either by connecting it to something else in your life that is already interesting to you or by creating your own intrigue through questions.

The Third Step: Activation

In a sense, you could say that this step is "when you start to learn". Of course, that is simplifying it a bit—but it can overall be viewed as when you are done with the "preliminary steps", and now are properly diving into the content of the topic at hand. Depending on the kind of learning that you are engaging with, this may be a video format, some sort of text you have to read through, physical hands-on work, or anything else that would fit the subject you are working with—and if that default format is what works best for you, then there is not much else that you have to do outside of starting your learning journey!

However, in the real world, not everything is always going to be as accommodating and fortunate as that at first glance; often, you will find that the format being presented for a diversity of interests will be equally diverse, and it is in that realm of difference where you may struggle. During the activation step of accelerated learning, while you are focusing more on the actual process of understanding, rather than the preliminary preparation of it, you *can* seek out better formats for the content if you find that the current methods are unhelpful for you. For instance, if you find that reading about something is not useful for your understanding, and a video lecture tends to bore you to the point where you cannot properly focus, then perhaps you could try to have a discussion about the topic with someone who knows better than you do? It is fine if you ultimately decide that the method you began with is the best choice after all; time spent trying to make your learning as exceptional as possible is not time wasted. Even if it ultimately brings you back to your starting point, you still *did* learn more about the subject at hand—and in a way that is especially useful if you ever want to help someone *else* understand more about the topic.

With the format of your education properly chosen, you will have to actually *do* the learning next. One trick that you can use to make sure that you are comprehending everything you are absorbing is to begin keeping a journal of what you are processing. In doing this, you can construct a framework that proves to yourself that you *are* understanding what is going on—and, more importantly, it will inform you of the gaps in your own knowledge, so that you can take the steps towards bridging said gaps. Another trick you can try is to make an actual physical "model" of what it is that you are trying to process; for instance, if you are attempting to understand the intricacies of one of Edgar Allen Poe's stories, you might assign one piece of paper to each character, and write what you know about them on their assigned page. The fact that you now have physical objects corresponding to these more intellectual, potentially abstract concepts can help ground them in your mind, helping you not only comprehend the information you have at hand better but also pick up new information and connections with greater ease.

Overall, activation is not exactly a *unique* step, as it could be argued that it is essentially both the start and end of traditional learning; yet that does not mean that it is a useless step by any means, because engaging with the work in some way *is* a requirement of learning, of course. Provided you are taking this step to make strides towards your education and do so with the method that suits you best, you will surely find success in it.

The Fourth Step: Demonstration

The best way to sum up this step would be through something that everyone has surely experienced in typical educational settings: an exam. Now, this does not have to be an actual proper multi-hour examination, one with a high-stress environment that requires an intense degree of focus—rather, this step is focused more on being a test of the skills that you have learned so far, to prove to yourself that you truly "get it" when it comes to your subject.

While the nuances of *how* you will demonstrate your knowledge depend significantly on both the scope of your goals and the individual topic that you are working with, there are still some key strategies that can apply to most. Writing a short summary is a common technique, making sure to not reference the original learning source while doing so—though, of course, examining your notes is just fine! Another way that you can examine your expertise is by trying to find problems based on the subject you are working with, and attempt to solve them; this is easier for a more typically problem-based subject, such as mathematics or chemistry, but with a bit of thinking you could very likely apply it to others! For instance, if you are working on improving your writing skills, perhaps you could find a challenging writing prompt for a scene that might be difficult to write a logical, satisfying conclusion for—and then, using what information you have gained from your training, do your best to create such a climax!

Of course, any sort of test would be faulty if it lacked guidelines; this is something that can logically stem from your ideas about your goals, as you figured out in both the first and second steps of the accelerated learning process. However, if you need to break down those ideas even further into more specific guidelines, then now is an excellent time to do so—ideally *before* you begin your demonstration.

Overall, the way that you handle demonstrating your prowess is just as subjective and personal as who the person learning is (you, of course) and the wealth of topics that can be learned; in other words, it is something that will require as much experimentation as anything else in this process would. Much like other experiments required for accelerated learning, you should attempt to create low-risk, high-reward experiences. You can do this by seeing which methods work best for you and determining what appeals to you the most as a showing of your newfound skills and then executing something that would be fine to experiment with. Such as learning a new dish when you already understand how to cook, or perhaps taking a crack at a new genre in a field of writing that you already know well enough. As long as you keep it relatively low-key and without risk, you can experiment during the demonstration step to your heart's content until you find a method that you feel is satisfactory enough to use "for real" with a more difficult subject.

To sum it up, this is your chance to prove to yourself that you understand what you have been learning and can actually do something with it. It is arguably one of the most "practical" phases and ignoring it would create the potential for learning flaws; for instance, it is like assuming you know how to play the piano after some practice, but then never actually playing a full song. While the nuances of this step will vary greatly, one thing is for certain: It is incredibly vital to keep in mind how you are going to demonstrate your knowledge.

The Fifth and Final Step: Consolidation

When it comes to practicing accelerated learning, if you have made it this far, then you are almost done; this is the last step of this process. In a sense, you have actually already "finished": The test was the Demonstration step, while this step is almost like an "epilogue" to what you have done—though it is still important, you can see it as having much less risk and far less stress than the rest of the process (although ideally, you should not be dealing with stress at all during the process). In a sense, you can look at this step as more so preparing you for the *next* time you engage in accelerated learning or the next time you engage with the topic at hand since these steps can be applied to the process of learning a single topic, in addition to attempting to master an entire subject.

First and foremost, as the name "consolidation" implies, you consolidate what you have learned; keeping a journal can be quite handy for this part of the process, as it not only serves as a way to remind you of things you might have forgotten, but it can also serve as an exploration of your knowledge journey, letting you see how far you have come. It might even give you a bit of a laugh to go back to it someday and find that topics that are so simple to you now were once, as recently as only a few months ago, difficult challenges. Regardless of *how* you consolidate the knowledge, it is important that you do so in a way that is easy for you to reference, and ideally, in some fashion that really hammers it home into your mind in one final way—while a written journal is effective, some learners find that an audio journal works better, or they record a video of some part of the process (such as painting a portrait).

After you have finished bringing all that you have learned together into one snug, fitting place, the next part of this step is to review— ideally not just by yourself, but also with others around you. In the most perfect circumstances, you have peers who are learning the same subject alongside you, so you can review with them; however, if you cannot, then you can always try to review with some experts to see if they can use their expertise in the topic to guide you along the right path. They can also help you in case there were any crucial steps you overlooked, or if they have any recommendations for your next step forward on the journey ahead. Another group you could review with could be as easy as finding a few of your friends: It might seem bizarre at first but reviewing with people who do not know much about a subject can actually grant an unbiased eye that might assist you in approaching the topic in another way. For example, if you talk with musicians about your studies of music, they might give you too specific advice while using musical jargon that might make you feel more confused. Meanwhile, if you were to discuss your music with someone else, they might point out that it "sounds like it just needs a little something here"; less specific, sure, but at times this can actually be better because it allows you to continue learning in ways that fit you best, while still giving you a nice set of guidelines to move along. Thinking for yourself is very important, after all!

During and after the review process, you should write down questions to look into in your next learning session; you might choose questions about the process itself (such as "Why did I decide to use physical blocks when I could have tried writing?"), or perhaps queries regarding the topic at hand (for instance "Why is it that writers do not often have characters explain exactly what they are thinking?"). If you have the chance to review with other people, then you should certainly let them ask questions—and if you cannot answer them, then that is the perfect chance for you to write them down alongside your own so that you can find the answers next time you delve.

Lastly, to finish off both this step and this chapter in general, you should do one final bit of pondering: What are you going to use this learning for? How will you integrate the techniques that you have studied the next time you are interacting with this subject? Will you take time outside to draw some birds rather than stick with still-life images? Are there genres that you have not yet written about, but now that you have learned more regarding those topics, you plan on giving them a try? Regardless of what your answer is, you have successfully taken the right steps towards learning what you wanted to, and so you cannot go wrong.

Chapter 5:

15 Powerful Approaches to Achieve Accelerated Learning

◆•————————•●•————————•◆

When it comes to approaching accelerated learning, there is a vast array of ways in which one can examine the learning process, enough to the point that just about anyone can find an approach that suits their individual needs best. In this chapter, I have compiled a list of 15 of the most effective tactics; while I have tried to be as comprehensive as possible, the main focus of my findings was to locate approaches that have been proven to be successful. Like all things with accelerated learning, you will need to experiment to find out which works the best for you, and so to make that part as easy as possible, I took it upon myself to research each and every one of these strategies in as much depth as I could, to guarantee that they are more than just theory craft; they are proven to work for the people that resonate with them most.

For The Self-Learner:
The Learner-Centered Approach

Arguably, this approach could be one that applies to *all* sorts of self-learning, since you would lack an educator other than yourself; as a result, I felt it best to get this one out of the way first. Rather than look at this as its own *unique* approach, it should best be perceived as a "modifier" you would add to any other approach, provided you either lack or do not want a teacher other than yourself.

When engaging in accelerated learning with a learner-centered approach in mind, you put the learner—likely yourself—in the direct focus of the education, allowing the individual to have more precise control over what sorts of information they are engaging with. As established by constructivist learning theory, one of the key principles of any sort of learner-central learning is the idea that knowledge must be at least partially created by learners themselves through constructing meaning out of the building blocks of experience, rather than just being something that can only be passively absorbed.

For the Fortunate:
Teacher-Based Approach

On the entire other end of the educational spectrum is the teacher-centered approach. Due to the self-help nature of this book, it is less likely that people who read this would have access *to* a teacher in their subject; however, if you do, then this sort of style can work wonders since it allows you to rely more heavily on the expertise that your instructor possesses, functioning like a springboard you can jump off from for your own learning.

As found by the University of San Diego, one of the most notable benefits of a learning style that focuses on the teacher is the idea of discipline or order: While there can be benefits to having more freedom in education, if you have the luxury of an instructor, it can be much easier for there to be an underlying structure. In regard to the lessons that you engage with, having a sense of structure—one that is personalized by your educator—allows the efficiency at which you can learn to be heightened significantly. After all, there is a great deal of focus that can be lost when trying to work out everything and having *too* much freedom.

The best way to sum up why this style is so effective for those who *can* afford to have an instructor is in one word: direction. If you know enough about your individual topic to the point where you can guide yourself in a solid direction independently, then this style is likely one you can pass over. However, if it is a topic that you are just now learning more about, then it can be extremely helpful to have a guiding hand along the way—even if just for the early steps.

The Multi-Dimensional Multi-Sensory Approach

In any sort of education, it is important to use your senses in some way; it might just be that you are using your sight to read, or your hearing to listen, but you are still using some sort of sense at the end of the day to process knowledge. Just using one or two senses is not enough to properly comprehend *everything* about the information being presented; however, there are ways to go much further and pick up said information with a greater degree of control, success, and understanding; using *all* of your senses—or at the very least *more* than just two.

As described earlier in this book, the brain works like a parallel processor, functioning at its absolute peak when it is trying to comprehend and work with a variety of different things; engaging as many of your senses at once as possible is one such way to put it into this hyper-stimulated overdrive. In a sense, you could compare this to how you might be able to remember the scenes of a movie better than a book; when it comes to work that is just text, you are only using your sense of sight, and only in its simplest form: Comprehending the words there, and then imagining what they mean.

For a film, on the other hand, you are engaging your eyes in a much more vibrant fashion, your ears are activated by the sounds of the scene going on, and you might even get a bit of "touch" if you are watching the movie in a theater, from the vibrations of the powerful speakers. All of this contributes to superior memorization of what happened, letting the information presented in those moments meld into your mind far easier than if it were just a book.

Collaboration as an Approach

While it is true that in public schooling you might see socialization discouraged during some moments of learning, viewing *all* sorts of social interaction as being "bad for your learning" would be inaccurate; in reality, the human mind is actually quite effective at processing information when we are enjoying ourselves, and as social creatures, humans tend to enjoy the company of others—especially when undergoing the same sorts of struggles and goals together.

Thus, if you use socialization in a collaborative approach—in the sense that you and your peers are all focusing on your collective learning, and are working together, rather than competing—then this is an immensely powerful perspective on education that can help you rocket along at high learning speeds. The effects of collaboration may vary from person to person. Experiment with this approach even more than all of the others to truly find the best results.

Visual Approach: Imagery Over Imagination

While it is true that I have already advocated multiple times for multi-sensory learning, it must be stated that sometimes people respond best to a single sense when it comes to certain topics; a visual-based approach may be difficult for trying to learn music, for instance, but if one is attempting to learn about visual arts, then it naturally tends to be one of the most effective strategies to use. As such, I would be remiss to avoid mentioning it and bringing up various ways that this sort of style can be used.

"Props" is a good word to describe what tends to be how visual approaches work; you have *something* that would be a fitting object for what you are learning, and you associate it with concepts. This can be more literal, such as the actual tool that you use for the techniques you are attempting to learn, or it could be more metaphorical, such as holding up a fork and studying its prongs when you are trying to learn how to make proper parallel lines. It is not exactly important how common the props are to find in your everyday life, or how often they are used by other people; what is integral is making sure that the symbolism sticks out to *you* specifically. Sometimes, it can actually be best if the props are more uncommon items, because they could be lacking in conflicting symbolism; thus, your mind can properly associate those images with the subject that you want to learn about.

Listening as an Approach: Active Engagement Through Audio

Much like how visual learning can be the best method for some who prefer to focus on a single sense, you can use your sense of hearing instead of sight if it suits you best. For the most part, the strengths of this approach tend to be the weaknesses of the visual style, and vice-versa—if you attempted to use visual learning in the past and found that it did not suit you or the topic you were engaging with, then attempting active listening would be my first recommendation!

The specifics of learning through listening were studied by Harvard University, where researchers found that the most effective approach was a more "active" one: Writing down questions, thinking independently as you process what you are hearing, and overall trying to process things beyond the "first thoughts" that you have ("The Value of Listening", 2017). For the best results possible, try to find some kind of audio source that you can replay and listen to more than once and then, listen to it the first time without taking too many in-depth notes—outside of a few questions you might have—and then listen to it again with much more in-depth notetaking. If you use this process, you will be able to digest the information much more effectively than if you just listened to it once and then never again.

Challenge-Based Learning: Knowledge Built through Struggle

For some individuals, the best way to push themselves and learn is by having specific obstacles to overcome. A study performed by the very aptly named website challengebasedlearning.org found that the most effective way to go about using an approach like this is through "breaking it up" when it comes to the subject; taking the pieces from the framework of the entire subject, and taking off smaller bits to turn into challenges for you to tackle head-on (Nichols & Cator, 2008).

Much like anything else when it comes to the learning process, the nuances will depend heavily on the topic that you are trying to engage with—but in general, you can approach creating challenges by making a series of guiding questions, such as asking yourself what the *purpose* behind each task is going to be, what it will end up teaching you to handle once you triumph over it, how you can engage with the challenge at hand, and so on.

This style of approach requires more effort than many other approaches, due to the very personal nature of conflict and challenge—but at the same time, it is through that higher level of effort that a greater understanding can be achieved for those who believe clashing with conflict as the ideal path to success.

The Verbal Approach of Reading and Listening

Commonly called the "verbal approach", the techniques found for this style are commonly used in the public education system. This style of learning is actually not exclusively listening, as one might imagine—a crucial difference between it and the typical listening approach is the fact that it involves significantly more reading. In a way, it can be thought of as the approach which values words above all; rather than wanting to be shown something, the individual instead prefers to have an explanation in words of some sort.

If you find that the verbal approach works for you, some strategies that you can do is by putting on closed captions while listening to a lecture and reading research papers, or academic textbooks.

Memory Learning

Memory is, of course, an important part of *any* kind of learning—you need to retain information to properly learn it, after all! However, despite that, there is also this approach to education that specifically *focuses* on the parts of the brain based on memory. In accelerated learning, one of the key tenets is the idea that knowledge is something the learner has to actively create through their experiences combined with the new information they process; this approach focuses more on this concept than any other.

As documented by Oregon State University (2019), the most effective way to engage with this learning style is to first try and use aspects of a different sort of approach to give you grounds to work with for your topic, and then to study in smaller pieces throughout the day. For instance, rather than doing one large 12-hour cramming session, you should split it up into four separate 3-hour study periods, with a sizeable break of at least 30 minutes between each. This concept, typically known as "distributing your practice", allows your brain to properly move what you are studying into your long-term memory while keeping your energy levels high enough to allow your studying to actually be effective. If you were to do that in a cramming session, you would burn out before long, making only the first half of it truly useful.

Active Learning: Making It Like a Game

One style which tends to be particularly effective is that of active learning. The techniques involved with this approach to education are about engaging you, the learner, in a way that has you actually *doing things*, rather than just sitting back and listening. Of course, to some extent *all* self-learning has aspects of activity—you would not have an instructor to teach you things themselves, after all—but there are differing degrees as to how far that is the focus of your learning.

Of course, being a more "broad" approach, there are a variety of ways in which you can engage yourself in your learning; as such, there are only two necessary parts to the active learning approach: You must be doing something which actively interacts with your mind, and, more crucially, you *must* still be able to learn through it. Some people find that video games work for engaging them for instance, but *does it still help you learn*? For some, it will, but for others it will actually serve to distract them from what they are meant to be learning, eliminating the purpose of using accelerated learning altogether!

Regardless of which method you find works the best for you, the hope of using this style is the fact that it makes you *want* to learn, and uses the parts of your brain that retain memory better through being interested and involved with your education.

The Experiential Approach

Accelerated learning is something that will require a good degree of trying out new things; it is a self-focused study, and the human mind is such a vast and subjective thing that it can be difficult to give a "one size fits all" suggestion for most areas. This approach plays a huge part in all of that.

The best way to describe experiential learning is almost like "surrounding yourself" with the topic that you are trying to learn more about; it is very much a "learn by doing" sort of style, and thus it really encourages you to throw yourself headfirst into the subject you're engaging with. For instance, if you are trying to learn how to write a book, the experiential approach to writing would be to actually go out there and write a book—one that is a lower-risk sort of story, like one you put online for free on some website, perhaps one that is not associated with your name, but still a book nonetheless. Northern Illinois University's Center for Innovative Teaching and Learning (2012) has used this technique to great success, outlining the process for how it can be applied to a more typical education; for someone who plans to be self-learning, the advice in this book is going to be more applicable, but their research is also excellent.

Looking Inwards with Reflective Learning

When it comes to any kind of skill set, you will need to examine where you are in terms of your abilities, how well the learning strategies you are using are working, and take an overall look at yourself in relation to your education. For the educational approach of reflective learning, this is heightened in importance; your ability to learn is based extensively on the data that you have gathered, testing it out in "the field", and then looking back and seeing how it went for you. To some extent, you could think of this learning approach almost like the "experimental" approach—not to be confused with the experiential approach, because although the two are similar, their nuances are very important to distinguish between in terms of what kinds of people benefit from each the most.

The most important difference between the two is the fact that, when it comes to reflective learning, you need to realize your weaknesses when it comes to the subject, and attempt to tackle them. For experiential learning, the learning process is *just* diving into the work and seeing how it is; for reflective learning, you also need to examine where your flaws are, and then focus on honing your skills all over until those flaws become negligible. This is the most self-critical of all of the learning approaches found within this book, and so it does not suit those who have difficulty criticizing themselves, or otherwise would be too dissuaded by doing so.

However, if you *are* the kind of person who is able to do so effectively, then this strategy has been found to be one of the absolute quickest. You can think of it like polishing a window: You can polish all of the easy-to-clean spots as much as you want, but if you do not attempt to tackle those harder smudges, then they will never come out. If the way that you are trying to clean is not working, then maybe just cleaning *harder* is not the right approach; you need to examine how you are doing things and figure that out rather than using a wet washcloth, you need to use some kind of spray on the dirt beforehand.

Metacognition: Learning Through Thinking About Your Thinking

To expand outwards in terms of direction, metacognition is almost like the learning approach *of* the learning approach; it is the sort of learning that is about learning itself. It can be argued that this is more of a strategy about which approach to pick rather than its own style; however, that is not necessarily true. When you use metacognition as your approach of choice, you work to think of a variety of strategies for each problem that you are tackling, and then you study each carefully beforehand, to make sure that it is the right way to go about things. This is also sometimes known as Bloom's Taxonomy when it is applied to the techniques that you are using for learning, especially in relation to examining typical studying techniques used in public education.

For a comparison to highlight why this is important, you can think of it like chopping down a tree. Imagine that you have a variety of tools at your disposal, and although most people would go for an ax, someone who does not know that much about how to do so might choose a spoon, a fork, or a knife. Certainly, jumping right in will save you time if you pick the ax—but not every problem you tackle will be as simple to figure out the right solution for as choosing an ax instead of a spoon would be. Instead, in this case, you would look at the four tools you have, highlight their characteristics, and come to the conclusion that the ax is the right choice—thus, you only spend a short amount of time with your metacognitive analysis, rather than wasting an entire workday because you tried to use a fork to stab a tree down. Thinking about your thinking is the most effective way to make sure your time is never wasted; it is *spent*, certainly, but it is an investment for your future, allowing you to use your time meaningfully.

Failure as an Approach: Understanding Mistakes and Pushing Onwards

Success is an important thing in our lives, being a driving force for many people—and of course, it would be, as the broad concept of "success" can essentially be applied to just about anything that anyone is trying to achieve. Yet, despite that fact, there are many who would see failure as something completely irredeemable, as if it could or *should* be avoided in its entirety.

An expectation like that is the antithesis of this learning approach. The truth about most things in life is that you *will* fail from time to time—if you expect perfection, then the majority of the time you will just be setting yourself up to fall short. Even if you ended up succeeding by the definition of the task, wanting perfection can still leave that mental wrinkle that you did not "succeed enough"— whatever that really means.

Failure, instead of being seen as some kind of monster to be evaded, is something that should be embraced. Of course, that does not mean you should *intentionally* fail; but rather, it is best to take your losses in stride, and examine every inch of them. It is not a bad idea to even try something you expect will fail in regard to your topic, such as trying a writing style infamous for its ability to seemingly never work, or creating a perpetual motion machine—because even though you believe you will not succeed, you can still learn a lot from the process itself. Plus, there is always the small chance that you *will* succeed at the end of the day, and in doing so you manage to create something unlikely, unexpected, and potentially quite wonderful.

Microlearning: Boiling It Down

To conclude this section on learning approaches is microlearning, the style that is perhaps most fitting for the end—it is last, and its style *is* least, however, its results are anything but. If I were to put microlearning in a word, it could be described best as "condensed"; it is a style that relies on compressing larger quantities of information down into pieces that are short, succinct, and easier to digest— almost like a "pill form" of what you are trying to understand.

While this style will likely sound the *most* appealing out of all—who does not want to save time, after all? It should also be clarified that it tends to work the absolute best by either turning the learning process into a game or through video formats. If you have seen any sort of 10-to-20-minute breakdown videos on a website such as YouTube, then that is the perfect example of what microlearning is; lots of information conveyed in a faster way to the point it can be absorbed in a reasonable amount of time. For using this approach, a significant amount of your self-education will rely on using videos like these (by *professionals*, ideally) or through some sort of educational game—as long as it is keeping everything concise and consistent, you will find that your brain can hold onto what you are learning far more than an overwhelming 5-hour lecture.

Regardless of which approach to learning you find works the best for you, hopefully, there is at least one that you find comes naturally. If you need to experiment, then that is just fine—it is all a part of the process! For any approach that you go for, the next chapter will brief you on different techniques which can be applied to all of these styles, allowing you to get more mileage out of your learning.

Chapter 6:

Efficient Techniques That You Can Use in Practice

At the point where you have reached this chapter, you should have some kind of approach figured out for how you want to use accelerated learning. It may be one of the styles recommended in the previous chapter, or it could be one that you have from a different source; the specifics do not matter, provided that it works for you. The contents you will find next are recommended techniques for use with any kind of approach to learning and should heighten your accelerated learning experience—with this knowledge in your hands, I hope that you will be able to learn anything you want at an efficient pace.

Being Deliberate with Your Practice

"Practice makes perfect." This is a mantra that has been repeated easily over a hundred times in your life, and it will likely be repeated a thousand times more after today—and to be honest, it is not necessarily incorrect! It is very important to practice because it hones the edge of your mind; you need to keep at whatever you are trying to learn, to transfer the knowledge from your short-term memory into your long-term memory, or to turn the thoughtful actions into reflexes—whatever it is that your individual subject or topic needs of you.

But it would be inaccurate to say that *all* practice makes perfect. In reality, bad practicing styles can actually be *worse* than not practicing at all, because they can make you feel as though you are a "loser", or that you "cannot learn anything right". Yet, the fault has nothing to do with you; instead, it is the fact that the method *in which you are practicing* is the mistake. This is not to claim that there is some kind of "miracle practice" which will let you understand the secrets of the universe after thinking for five seconds and nothing else; there will still be work to be done, of course, like in all things. However, if you arm yourself with the knowledge of how to *properly* practice, then you can actually make some headway with your preferred subject, instead of what feels like bashing your head on a brick wall.

As defined by Learning Sciences International, doing a practice that is deliberate can best be summed up as identifying specific skills to be exercised, rather than vague concepts, and then practicing them in an intense manner (Marx, 2022). An important point to note is that while this is the "practice" part of deliberate practice, there is also an essential aspect that you cannot go without targeted feedback. If you have any sort of peer group, then it can be beneficial to have them give you feedback; if not, you will have to rely on your own judgment when it comes to critiquing your education. Either way, rather than general talking points for how to improve, it is best to outline the *specifics* as much as you can—if you have peers, you can ask them questions such as how you can improve in a specific area, highlight techniques that you feel that you were struggling with, or otherwise try to pinpoint specific struggles to tackle. If you do not, you can instead ask these questions to yourself; it may be difficult to answer some of them, but if you look through the learning resources you have available to you, it should be feasible.

After you have received feedback, you should turn the suggestions into a plan of action—for most people, it works best to outline a multi-step plan for how to proceed forwards. For instance, if there was feedback about how your drawings of people have issues regarding anatomy, you might make the first step be about head shapes or the angles at which you draw hands. The most important aspect of how you structure this plan is the fact that it works for you and will give you a clear objective for how to proceed; if you make it too vague, then that haziness can create difficulties when it comes time to actually getting back to the learning process.

Provided you are willing to commit to the learning process and can entice yourself to remain deliberate throughout the entirety of your practice, this first technique on the path to accelerated learning should serve as a guiding force to propel you forwards through the rest.

Interleaved Practice: Alternating Skills

When it comes to most topics, there is a variety of skills you can learn, rather than just a single way to tackle every facet of the subject. For instance, if you are trying to learn how to draw, you cannot *just* learn linework and that is it: you also have to understand concepts about shading, anatomy, and color. Most people would believe that the best way to go through these different techniques would be to focus until you understand one *entirely*, and then move on to the next. However, the University of California San Diego's Department of Psychology conducted research into the topic and discovered that it actually was more efficient to bounce between different nuances in the topic, rather than remain on one for a longer period of time ("Self-Explanation, Interleaved Practice, and Other Learning Techniques", n.d.).

This technique for learning, usually called "interleaved practice" (although alternating practice is another acceptable name), relies on learning two or more concepts in the same learning period. There are two distinct styles of how that is done: A more "true" alternating style, going back and forth between the ideas, or you can attempt to mix what you are learning about them together; for instance, instead of just writing a practice story that exclusively focuses on how you handle one style of character, you can also use that same story as a way to work on your ability to write background descriptions. This can allow each bit of knowledge that you acquire to work almost like a chain-link fence; having these ideas divided would allow you to have gaps in your understanding, but by interleaving them together, their bonds become a much stronger force that allows you to use one part of your memory to access the rest of it.

One issue that can be found through the use of this strategy is the fact that it can make the actual practicing portion difficult; you may find that what was once mindless repetition can become something requiring significantly more thought and focus. However, while you may lose some bits of relaxation at first, it has been shown through studies such as the one conducted by Doctor Taylor and Doctor Rohrer (2010) that even if there *are* negative effects on the practice session, when it comes to actually applying the information that you have learned, interleaving practice shows much greater success than what might have been expected. It may be a struggle at first to push through practice when first attempting to weave different skills together, but it is worth a significant amount of time to try it—an investment for your future, both in your ability to keep the information that you try to absorb and in shortening the total length of your practice sessions. In time, you may find that interleaved practice can become just as relaxing as more typical study sessions—all you need to do is keep trying at it, and "practice your practice", so to speak.

Practice Through Testing Yourself

While you may find aspects of success in practicing endlessly, you can only truly accomplish your goals by actually doing things; knowledge that is just sitting around in your head, doing nothing, can eventually rot away until you have lost it all. Yet, at the same time, it would be risky to just practice and then immediately jump into a situation that demands you know your best, without *any* assurance that you have actually been tested before.

The ideal method to solve this dilemma is by testing yourself in a low-risk fashion. There is a variety of methods that one can use to go about this; flashcards are one of the most common ways that people do this, and it is very likely that *you* have done so yourself. If the skill that you are learning is one that is typically more academic, you could also attempt some review quizzes online on various websites—and even if the subject is not as popular, or it would be too specific to your style of learning to use such tests made by other people, you can always make your own! Creating your own risk-free exams can be done through any website of your choice, or even doing it by using pen and paper; after you have made it, using various questions that will truly test your knowledge, you should wait a few days so that the knowledge is a bit less at the forefront of your mind. Then, if you come back to the test and can still answer everything confidently and correctly, it shows that you are able to bring that information back to the surface!

When it comes to however you end up testing yourself, it is very important that in the sorts of questions you are asking you avoid overtly recognition-based content—such as multiple-choice questions, which tend to ask you not what you actually *know*, but instead rely on the vaguest recollections of what you can and cannot identify. What *is* recommended are tasks that require greater amounts of mental retrieval, as such tests will be more accurate to practical use for skills; certainly, self-testing that is based on recognition can work sufficiently if the only reason that you are learning something is for academic testing. But, if you want to actually use the skills you are studying in your life, the style known as "free recall" is significantly better than true and false tests.

Another powerful strategy that some experts recommend is called "elaborative interrogation", which can be thought of like a conversation or debate that you have with yourself, in which you ask yourself to define the concepts that you are learning, and then further delve into why it is that the knowledge you are learning is true. As an example, you might be learning about baking, and could ask yourself why it is that having something in the oven for 10 minutes longer than the recipe calls for is a disaster; you may have some practical experience to support the fact that it could ruin what you are baking, or maybe you could have a greater understanding of the chemical compounds which would be disrupted by the excessive amount of cooking time. Provided you have an actual answer, the kind that can properly convince you that it is the matter-of-fact truth, then you know what you are talking about; if you cannot provide such an answer, then it is likely reason for you to take another dive back into the topic.

Overall, regardless of how you choose to test yourself, provided you do it regularly and with discipline, you can retain the knowledge that you have worked so hard to obtain in the first place.

Retrieval-Based Learning: Bringing It All Back

If you look into your memories from just a little while ago, you should recall that in the last section, the idea of mental retrieval was mentioned. This concept is what you just used right there—at least, in a more low-risk, short-term sort of fashion. While it can suffice as just one example of the idea of retrieving memories for the sake of education, there are much more detailed ones that could be used; still, having that sort of personal experience with the topic felt necessary to show the importance of it.

A study conducted by Doctor Karpicke (2008, p. 967) in *Science* journal made use of four different groups who were learning a foreign language, changing how they handled terms after they were shown to have the capability to identify them. The first group continued to study the term and had regular tests for it, functioning as a sort of "control" group; the second group studied as well, but it was dropped from all further examinations. The third group was the exact opposite of the second, no longer studying any ideas that they had processed before, but those same terms were still brought up in tests. The last group dropped the concept entirely, never bringing it back up in any capacity—no studying nor testing. Surprisingly, while the first group performed well, as you might expect, the third group actually had very similar results—better than the second and fourth by a significant margin.

Studies like this allow us to look deeper into ideas relating to how people learn, and apply them to our own lives; thus, we can create accelerated learning opportunities. This experiment shows the effectiveness of practicing with mental retrieval: Instead of focusing on studying over and over, you should place yourself in environments that allow your skills to come up more naturally, even if it might be a more stressful scenario. This can be very similar to the concepts laid out in the self-testing section of this chapter, but it should be noted that there is a greater degree of "practical experience" with this: You should avoid ideas related to flashcards and other similar studying resources, in favor of just using your mind and taking on tests that rely more on your mind alone.

Of course, you are also free to make use of *both* of these practice techniques if you find that their shared benefits would be helpful to your specific topic. At the end of the day, your own judgment will be an important deciding factor when it comes to which parts of this book are useful to you, and which tidbits of knowledge might be better suited for someone else; the best that I can do is give the greatest advice that I can.

Spreading Out Studying Through Spaced Repetition

Despite what you may have gathered from the other practice strategies outlined in this chapter, studying is not *inherently* a bad thing; really, to some extent, you have to do *some* amount of studying to have information to test yourself on. The human brain is a wonderful and unique thing, and what works for one brain *may* work for another—but there is just as high a chance that it will not. For those of you who find studying to be quite effective, this technique is just for you; for those who do not, at least take some solace in knowing this advice might make those difficult study sessions into something more palatable.

If you look at just about anything discussing student life, *especially* in regard to university learning, you will certainly see at least one mention of "cramming"—extremely rapid studying condensed into a small, high-stress period. There are a thousand ways that someone could tell you that this does not work; rather than do as so many others have, I would like to dedicate this section of the chapter to outlining an alternative solution you can use. Instead of having fewer study sessions that are individually quite long, you can instead make use of spaced repetition: shorter periods where you are studying, but having them frequently, reliably, and relatively regularly.

As outlined by Doctor Ausubel and Doctor Youssef (1965) in a study conducted for *The Journal of General Psychology*, the effects of spaced repetition are quite notable on the learner's ability to meaningfully retain the information regarding their subject. As they and others have found when a group has their repetition spaced out in periods of at least 48 hours, their ability to remember their topic is heightened significantly compared to those who studied it every single day. This is sometimes known as the *spacing effect*, and mastering it is key in making sure that your hours studying are not wasted—if you just keep pushing yourself to try and learn what you can every single day, you will find your mind burning out, unable to retain *anything*, much less the important parts of your work. However, if you make sure to give yourself regular breaks, and space your studying out across multiple days, dedicating certain days to breaks, you will be able to process your subject significantly more than if you just kept at it recklessly.

Of course, a natural issue that arises when trying to use this strategy is the fact that the purpose of accelerated learning tends to be to learn *faster*; as a result, if there is a larger amount of content you need to get through, then this technique may not work as well for you. However, it can still be applied to the most integral concepts of your topic! For instance, you might go over the important details of how to write the end of a story with proper theming once every three days, while the rest of the writing process you learn about each day. This would allow you to increase your general skills for your subject while keeping the important concepts more firmly in your mind; if you use this alongside interleaved practice (as described earlier in this chapter), you can extend that heightened memory to the rest of what you are learning.

Overall, the degree to which you should make use of this technique will depend heavily on the exact nature of why you are using accelerated learning, and that is something that you will have to decide for yourself. If you can afford to space out your learning over a longer period of time, then this is just the technique for you; if you cannot, then you will more than likely find greater success with one of the other techniques listed in this chapter.

Chapter 7:

Creative Techniques That You Can Use for Asking Questions

When it comes to self-education, one aspect that you will have to have sufficient skills for is asking questions. In traditional education, you have a teacher of some sort who can ask all of the questions—all the students have to do is answer them, without forming their own queries. Yet, when you lack someone else to guide you, the person who ends up asking all the questions that the educator would, becomes the learner themselves—in this case, that would be you. As a result, you need to know how to ask the *right* questions; you can ask yourself what 2 + 2 is every single day for years on end, but if that's *all* you do, you'll never be able to understand advanced geometry.

This chapter contains four strategies that you can make use of when asking questions so that you can properly take the right steps forward when it comes to your learning.

Asking Questions Through Analogical Thinking

Analogical thinking, also known as relational thinking, is a flexible mentality based on creating connections between different situations and parsing them together—analogies, in other words. It is a crucial part of human psychology and problem-solving, allowing us to see situations that we have never experienced before, compare them to scenarios that we have dealt with in the past, and come up with a solution based on our previous knowledge.

For the sake of accelerated learning, this psychological tool remains ever-useful—but it must be reverse-engineered for the sake of self-education. Rather than trying to solve a new problem, you are working to *create* a question. This can be exceptionally challenging because when it comes to the creation of questions for self-education, it has to be a problem that you could feasibly solve—either with the information that you currently possess or by studying further to gain what is required—but not yet one that you already know the answer to. This sort of higher-order thinking is integral to accelerated learning, and so although it may be difficult, it is imperative to understand how it relates to your individual subject of study.

To give an analogy of how best one could use analogical thinking, visual art is a sufficient example; you might already understand how to draw shadows when it comes to work that you draw with a pencil, especially in monochrome color schemes. However, if you were to start painting, and make use of color, then you would not only have to understand how differing hues interact with shadows, but how the very medium of paint conquers the question of how to make shadows appear. Though there will be aspects that will only be understood through more research and self-testing, you can at least think of how to shade with a pencil, then apply it as best as you can to your art with a brush.

Some of the comparisons that you will have to make may transfer less literally, such as understanding plumbing through your experience composing music—but if you are able to make *any* sort of connection, and create an analogy that makes sense to *you*, then that is all that matters. It is fine if the way that they connect sounds insane to someone else; provided that it works the most important factor is the fact that it functions for you. When you assume the role of your own educator, there will always be bizarre choices that you have to make based on your own understanding of what works best for your individual learning process, and this is no different.

Condensing Knowledge Through Behavioral Psychology

One of the most challenging things when it comes to any new task is that it can have overwhelming expectations. If you look at most masterfully crafted paintings, there will be so many steps that you have to know how to do properly to create such a thing. You have to understand how to use colors effectively to convey the scene that you want, you need to know how to properly construct figures so that they match the overall shape of your intentions, and you need to understand value, depth, shading—the number of concepts that an artist has to process can seem endless. When you look at a masterpiece such as the *Mona Lisa,* doubts certainly creep in for many, telling the person that they "can't do it", that they "aren't good enough", or that there's "too much to learn".

Behavioral psychology provides a tool for understanding our ability to learn overwhelming topics like this, unlocking our own self-inflicted chains. It is a quite simple technique one can use, but one that is surprisingly effective, as well: Breaking things down into smaller steps.

Going back to the example of the *Mona Lisa*, perhaps you want to know how to paint something that captivates you but find it too difficult to even start to comprehend how you would do so. Rather than begin with trying to recreate the whole; instead, think of replicating the individual steps that you need to take—perhaps first try to draw a head or a hand, or start working on painting the background before anything else. Maybe you want to work on something similar, but not necessarily a replica of the same painting; the same applies there, too. Just take a few deep breaths and work out the individual bits that make up the whole, then do your best to understand how to paint those parts.

Mentally, you need to summarize your goals into these bite-sized steps, and then it can all seem significantly easier to manage. Rather than thinking about a book as "writing an epic 80,000-word novel about the political ideology of an empire of robots powered by rodents and solar power", create a plan for how you will handle the first chapter, the important details of the main character, the structure of the first page—nothing is too small, provided that it gets you *started*. The most difficult step you take during a marathon is the very first, and while there will always be that temptation to sprint, you have to keep at a steady pace if you want any hope of actually finishing it.

Single-Loop Learning:
Receiving and Applying Feedback

When it comes to any learning method, there will always be challenges in making sure that you are learning in a way that actually suits your needs; it *is* possible that the tutorial you found online for *how to cook using an oven* will have aspects that could apply to doing so with your toaster oven, but that would be a risk that relies more on assumption than fact. Rather than doing that, you could instead examine the situation and see how best to improve what information is being supplied to you in the first place—finding a *proper* tutorial for your toaster oven, rather than relying on one for a stovetop or other kind of oven.

This line of organizational thinking is known as "single-loop learning" since it relies on a single repeated feedback loop: Engaging in the learning process, receiving feedback on how you are learning (either from yourself, your peers, or an instructor), and then altering the educational process itself. Ideally, when using this technique, you only need to engage with the loop once or twice, so that you can continue with your understanding with as few unnecessary stops as possible. However, that is something that is going to depend not only on the individual subject, but also on your ability to parse the subject's concepts, the nature of how experimental the work you are doing might be, and any other relevant factors which would apply to the skills that you are learning.

Ultimately, this line of organizational thinking is important when it comes to trying to alter your educational routine and doing so in a way that can be relatively quick. Due to the fact that this book focuses on accelerated learning, it becomes an obvious choice for a method of asking questions; granting a clear goal for those questions—how you should alter the process to finish the feedback loop—and in the most optimal circumstances, the process for it is quick, easy, and painless. Yet, for certain subjects, this version of organizational feedback loops is actually suboptimal, and can end up wasting more time than it saves; for such a topic, you need to instead go forth with a technique that can be slower in the short-term, but better in the long-term.

Double-Loop Learning: Less Risk, More Time, More Reward

Single-loop learning is defined as such because it involves a very linear process in how it alters your learning: constant incremental change. Its speed can be quite beneficial, because a single isolated loop, or even a handful of loops, will not typically take up a large amount of time; the way that they are altering how you do things can be minute or grand, but it still stays on the overall track that you began on, and as such the changes that you implement tend to be smaller.

However, it is not a perfect process. Imagine you are trying to make a drawing that you want to be full of vibrant colors, with deep crimsons and verdant greens, picturing all of the colors in your head and knowing exactly what it is that you want to do with it all. You buy a bunch of pencils, and find that no color is coming from them; if you were to use single-loop learning, then you would not be changing the overall process (using the pencils), but instead incrementing towards differing in your methods—maybe you might try to draw *differently* with the writing tools, or break them apart, perhaps use some shavings of the eraser in an attempt to get more colors. It is possible that this could create a work of art that is similar to what you wanted, or that it could even reveal a new style of doing things that you prefer much more.

But it is overwhelmingly more likely that it would have been a better idea to just buy some *colored* pencils instead. Double-loop learning involves the exact same steps that single-loop learning does, but it also includes a secondary cycle of feedback as part of its core loop, where you examine the procedure, you have standardized itself, questioning if *that* needs to change as well.

If everyone had endless time, then certainly there would never be any reason to make use of single-loop learning styles—because the only real downside to using double-loop over single-loop is the passage of time. However, that is not the world that we live in—and so, if you are to use either of the looping styles to ask questions about your process, you need to determine how much time you can afford to spare. If you are able to spend a larger quantity of time on the subject and are fine with slowing down your pace to attempt to improve the way you are learning overall, then using the double-loop method is superior; if you do not have such luxury, then single-loop would be your best bet. All of it is a gamble at the end of the day, at least to some extent, and the best you can do is try to minimize the risk and maximize the reward.

Regardless of which method in this chapter you find works best for you, or if you even have a strategy entirely different from what was outlined above, it must be stated that the ability to properly ask questions about how your learning process is going is integral for self-education. Accelerated learning applied to self-education focuses on this more than typical self-education since speed is of the essence and personal differences in learning style can be more pronounced when the process is accelerated. Still, the process of asking yourself questions to proceed with self-lead education is something that will apply to *any* form of personal education—so even if you find that accelerated learning did not suit your needs, you should at least keep some of the advice contained in this book in mind.

And if I were to pick any chapter, in particular, to be kept in mind, I would certainly choose this one.

Chapter 8:

Techniques Applicable for Association

◆•————————●————————•◆

The human brain is a fantastic organ that allows us to function in the world with a higher level of cognition—it could be said that it is what separates humans from all other creatures of the world that we live in. If it were a perfectly functioning device, learning would be a much easier process for us all; we would not have to deal with issues and errors from the gaps in our own psyche.

Now, for a little exercise, think about the person that you last spoke with and in your mind, do your best to picture their pinky finger—and nothing else. When you try to do this, you think about their hand, their arm, and it likely extends to the point where you can think about the rest of the person, but maybe struggle with parsing the nuances of their pinky finger. This is a principle known as "associative learning", based on concepts of how the mind perceives the world, linking experiences and objects together, rather than having them "float" away from one another as isolated thoughts.

This is a good thing—or, at the very least, it can be made into one. Going back to the example of the pinky finger, if you were to *consciously* focus on that person's pinky the next time you met them (which perhaps you should not, as they might find that quite bizarre), then repeat this exercise, you would find that the details would come much more naturally. Part of why it was likely challenging to imagine the intricacies before was because, in all likelihood, you have not thought very much of people's pinkies in general.

Something else you might take note of is the fact that you remember the *other parts* of that person's hand with better accuracy; that focus you placed upon the pinky naturally made you mentally jot down the surrounding details with greater precision than before. What you learned by doing this exercise is also applicable to other forms of study.

Human Associative Learning: Socializing for Skills

There are two camps of associative learning techniques which can be applied broadly to any subject; the first of these is known as "human associative learning" and can otherwise be thought of as associative learning through socialization.

Think about a speech that you have heard—either directly, perhaps through a movie, or even in writing. When you have it in mind, certainly the speech itself is front and center; yet the speaker that gave the speech is also going to be relevant in your mind, are they not? The same can apply inversely—who would think of Doctor Martin Luther King Junior without immediately having his "I Have a Dream" speech in their thoughts within just a few moments? It is certainly possible that his speech was great enough for many to remember without it being associated with the man—if it were just written down on a piece of paper and published without a face to put it to, or if it were inscribed on a monument made by an unknown artist.

But I am certain you will find that having a well-known figure to associate it with makes the recollection of that knowledge so much easier. This is not just something that has to be exclusively reserved for the famous, powerful, and respected; the people in your life, from the heroes that you look up to, to your friends that you interact with daily, can be excellent associations for the skills that you want to master.

If you have any peers learning alongside you, then those are naturally the first people that come to mind; it might be a struggle for you to remember how to write a compelling villainous character arc on your own, but if you think about how a friend of yours does that in all of their stories, then you can remember the steps that they took to do so and apply parts of it to your writing. It does not have to be a direct association through that person's individual skills, either—something that you can do to mentally "trick" yourself into associating aspects of your learning with other people is through having a conversation with them.

As another example, do you usually watch movies with other people, or do you prefer to be by yourself? For the films that you watched on your own, how well can you recall aspects of the plot? Most likely there are some details that come to mind, but there is a good possibility that you might even forget which film it was until it suddenly pops into your mind. In comparison, when you watch a movie with other people and then talk about it with them, not only will you find that they point out details you did not realize, *but* the discussion itself will remain in your mind much easier—and thus, you retain that information about the experience with greater success.

Now, I would like to clarify, I am not advocating for *using* other people as if they are tools or keeping them in the dark about this; certainly, if someone is a celebrity, and your mental association with them and the skill you are learning is more in a "role model" sense, there might not be means nor reason to let them know. However, for the people in your life, it is best to let them know that you wish for their aid, even if just by association—telling them this will allow them to actively assist you in whatever way they want to. This can include a more direct connection, such as them imparting the knowledge they have about the subject—but, of course, every single person is unique, and so the exact ways in which they might help will differ. With all things in this book, as I have tried to stress this point that experimentation is key—though hopefully not to the point of repeating myself too frequently.

But perhaps associating your knowledge with others is not the best method for you. It certainly is possible that none of the people in your life would be relevant to the line of work that you want to learn more about—or maybe it is a skill that you want to keep a surprise for whatever reason, such as to use for making a birthday gift for someone. Whatever your reason, there is another quite potent method of association that many individuals have found success with.

Location Association:
Experiences to Educate

In our modern world, being educated exclusively in a single topic is certainly rarer compared to how it might have been centuries ago—while people are more likely to be an expert in just one subject, most will still have at least a passing comprehension of entirely unrelated topics. Think about the different subjects that you have learned, and more specifically, try to remember where you learned these concepts—for most self-learners, it was likely in the same location. Perhaps it was the same for you; places like your desk at home, a local library, or maybe even a nice coffee shop—all fine places to learn, all things considered.

Yet, if you are studying *every single topic* in the *exact same location*, an issue can come to mind: It all tends to bleed together. It is true that this chapter has so far been about the benefits of associative learning—but it cannot be understated that associating too much with the exact same stimulus can drown out the older topics. This tends to be part of why it is that movies or books that juggle too many characters and plot threads can be unremarkable and difficult to remember; your mind is unable to grasp onto a solid foundation simply because there is too much, creating a form of analysis paralysis in regard to your memory.

Therefore, it is actually best to try and go to a different location for each subject you want to study—even just a different room of your house will work, such as learning about art in your living room or a studio, and cooking in your kitchen. By separating the subjects you are learning like this, it will naturally be easier to remember details about the topic when you are either in that room or one that is similar; if you usually make tea using a kettle, for instance, then seeing a similar kettle out in the world would bring to mind information about tea.

Now, the association here, just like with people, does not have to be direct; you could go to a movie theater and use the experience to learn about woodcarving, head to a library that your brain will associate with death metal music, or a coffee shop to understand the taxonomy of parts of the animal kingdom. The only tenets that are important are that you are able to *consistently* associate it with your subject of study, that it can be a place free of distractions, and that the location is one that you can reliably revisit when you need to refresh your memory on the topic at hand. Of course, the last one can be a bit more challenging depending on circumstances—but it can also be substituted; while you might not be able to access a specific camping ground at any time during the year, you could at least head somewhere that is full of similar sights, like a park with lush greenery. For most people, that should be enough to bring about proper associative memorization.

Visual signifiers are also an important puzzle piece when it comes to location-based connections—as mentioned above, plants such as oak trees can be an effective symbol since they are easy enough to locate for most people but *just* rare enough that you can link the sight of them to aspects of knowledge. Regardless of what visual signifiers you end up using, it does not have to be something native to that area, provided you can associate it in some other way; for instance, if you choose to study music at a coffee shop, you more than likely would not be able to bring an entire set of drums with you and play them in the establishment. However, you could end up using two plastic knives like makeshift drumsticks, tapping them on the table to try and improve your sense of rhythm; thus, you have created the visual signifier of plastic knives used as drumsticks. By holding those objects and being in a cafe or other similar location, you can put your mind in a "flow" state which would heighten the comprehension of the music you want to learn about, almost like flipping a "learning mode" switch in your mind.

Of course, it might all sound very silly on the surface, as if it is something that would be used for a child—but even if it might be a little bit silly, children tend to be the best at absorbing information, are they not? Therefore, I think that there is some credence in understanding the world through a lens that reflects that of young learners.

Regardless of which associative learning techniques you find function the best for you, something to keep in mind is that they do not have to be mutually exclusive; you can have a learning experience in a specific location, and then have a conversation about that experience with someone in your life. In fact, by doing so, you can create a feedback loop that associates the person and the place together, and the knowledge interlinked between them; doing this when you want to master a *variety* of topics could potentially create complications, due to the aforementioned over-association. However, if you plan on using accelerated learning for only a few areas of study, then this strategy of combining the two kinds of associative learning can be extremely effective.

PILLAR 5:

EDUCATIONAL DESIGN

Chapter 9:

Smart Systems to Learn Fast

When it comes to all of the techniques outlined in this book, one thing that should not be forgotten is the overall purpose of this collection of knowledge: accelerated learning. In particular, the want to process and absorb information at a faster pace than you did before—for which, of course, all of the previous chapters have given ample applicable advice. However, the degree of customizability that has been offered creates the potential to "lose" something; the degree of speed at which you can work might be lowered, specifically when testing the variety of suggestions against one another, trying to find the most effective method to follow.

This chapter contains tried-and-true systems created by accomplished people—guaranteed to let your learning soar. All of the suggestions contained earlier in this book can be combined with this collection of strategies at your preference; this is not to say that you have wasted your time reading the previous chapters of this book, but instead that you should look at these systems as templates.

Luhmann's Zettelkasten System

If one were, to sum up Niklas Luhmann's Zettelkasten in one word, it would be "efficiency". It is a system of notetaking, one which could best be compared to creating your own personal Wikipedia for your mind, enabling you to have clear guidelines and access to all of the knowledge in your mind at once. Though, it is a method that can take some time to set up, since it is essentially emulating the kind of computer software known as a "hypertext" on your own, the results grant a blindingly fast boost to your information comprehension.

First and foremost, you will want to begin taking notes on your subject—the original Zettelkasten system makes use of paper notes, and many find that using physical paper improves their ability to keep it in mind. Still, digital notes can also suffice if they work for you. After that, you need to make sure that the notes are given "addresses"; more specifically, each independent note has a number attached to it, and then for dependent notes, you add a letter. If that dependent note receives a note of its own that relies on it, but is not continuing that exact train of thought, then you would put a number, then a letter if that one receives one—and so on and so forth.

This creates a system where you might have "main notes" notes with the addresses of 1, 2, 3, 4, and 5, and then thoughts relating to the expansion of those notes with addresses of 1a, 1b, 2a, 5a—continuing on for as long as is required for both your individual subject and personal thought process. Using this style of notetaking allows for more organic growth through your notes, rather than the rigidity that many other systems tend to fall prey to—a mistake that goes against how the human brain works with knowledge.

The way that it is defined as a "hypertext" is because it is self-referential; using the Zettelkasten method requires some set-up beforehand, because you will need to write out concepts you know, in terms that you understand, and in ways that you can reference later. However, while it will have that starting procedure, the fact that you will not have to pull out books and search through the pages will speed up your learning in the future—even for a task that would require you to cite your research (such as with writing), you could simply list the sources in one of the notes itself so that you do not need to pull it out manually.

Despite the fact that Luhmann's Zettelkasten was created quite a while ago, it is still a shockingly modern system and one that many online databases to this very day are based on. If you end up applying it to your own knowledge, you will be surprised at how efficient it is for information recollection.

The Sönke Ahrens Method

The Sönke Ahrens method for note-taking—otherwise known as the "Ahrens method" or "smart notes"—makes use of digital tools and the concept of a "slip box" to create notes in a fashion that could almost be described as diegetic. An argument that he makes, one which is key to understanding the nature of smart notes, is the idea that beginning a writing project with a blank piece of paper is the first step towards failure; instead, note-taking must not only be done as a formality but as a guiding hand done before any work is done at all, so as to create a proper outline.

Using a slip box is not unique to the Ahrens style of note-taking—in fact, it is what the Zettelkasten described above makes use of quite heavily as an externalized way for organizing notes. The key difference is in the idea of nonlinear thinking, and how an individual should apply that to the notes that they are taking. The best way to properly explain and describe what linear thinking would refer to in this context is, as defined by Ahrens: Having a preconceived "goal" for the research that you are undertaking.

Let's say that you wanted to prove that gravity is fake, despite what everyone else claims—something exceptionally bold, but if you were to look, then you could potentially find evidence that would corroborate that argument. For instance, bees are able to fly, even though their general anatomy seems to disagree with that; gravity, supposedly, would prevent them from flight despite their weight and wingspan. Despite all that, the bee is able to take flight; thus, this proves that gravity is not real—at least when approaching research in an extremely linear fashion.

In reality, the issue here lies within the fact that there was a notion already planted in the researcher's mind—"gravity is fake"—and rather than look at the evidence which broadly relates to how gravity does or does not function, they instead looked exclusively for exceptions to the rule to try and prove the entire system wrong. As a result, not only did this fashion of thinking ignore all of the evidence proving that gravity is real, but it additionally ignored information regarding how bees are able to fly allowing them to "bypass" gravity—which they do not, but instead, their method of flight is just *different* from most other animals.

To avoid an error like this, you would need to make a list of works to examine based on their subject, and approach it with an unbiased lens—compile *all of the arguments*, rather than just the talking points which specifically prove a pre-existing goal. Afterward, it can be placed in a slip box in a similar fashion to the Zettelkasten, allowing you to access that information at a later date with a more unbiased viewpoint; you are now able to understand the entirety of the situation, rather than just a single narrow scope of the subject, all through looking at the topic with a bird's eye view.

SQ3R: Survey, Question, Read, Recite, and Review

Unlike many of the strategies highlighted in this book so far, this is one that comes from the public education system. Primarily, it is used for texts full of exposition, but the comprehension skills that are granted by this technique are ones that can be applied to alternative self-education styles. SQ3R is a very literal name, coming from the five steps of this process: survey, question, read, recite, and review. This method is particularly useful if you find that you are an adept reader—though it can still be useful otherwise, if reading is your preferred way to learn, then I cannot recommend any technique higher than this one.

Survey

Before you begin reading the "meat" of a text, you should first begin by gathering the knowledge about the work itself to help you proceed forwards in the most effective way. If there are any reading aids or other tools provided by the book (such as a glossary), then you should attempt to locate those and keep them in mind; ignoring them might lead to unnecessary confusion. When you start reading the actual work, focus especially on the title and introduction—what do they tell you about what you are going to read? Are there any necessary points that will be integral to your understanding?

Overall, this step allows you to process what is coming ahead, that way you may continue with exceptional efficiency; to ignore it would be to risk having multiple stopping points, cutting off all momentum that you had beforehand.

Question

For the next step, when you begin reading a chapter or section of the work you are engaging with, you should ask questions about what you are immediately presented with (ideally writing them down). For instance, you might ask yourself about the chapter's name, and make some guesses about what contents might be in store as you read further. This could seem a bit pointless, but it is important for preparing your mind properly to absorb the information coming ahead—the brain processes knowledge better when it feels actively engaged, and asking questions such as these is the simplest way to energize those aspects of your psyche.

This second step is one that lets you properly slip into the "learning phase", allowing you to face learning head-on with confidence and curiosity. It is imperative to follow this step so that you can proceed with grace and efficiency.

Read

It may be difficult to understand the heading of this section, but you are required to read for the reading step—I know, I know. To go into a bit more detail: This step is not just about reading, but also a bit of writing—in fact, you should write down the answers to the questions that you had up to this point, once their solutions have come to pass. If you did *not* end up writing down your questions, then you could try to mentally take note of the answers as well;

however, once more, it is highly recommended that you *do* write them down, as they serve as a guide for later.

Since this step is less about strategy and more about the actual procedure of *beginning to learn*, this is *the* most important part of SQ3R; without doing it, you never began in the first place.

Recite

When you finish a section—such as a scene in a story, or a sub-section in an educational textbook—try to answer the questions you initially prepared; not from looking at your written notes, but just from your memory alone. If you are unable to, consider reviewing the section again. Afterward, you may move on to the next section of the work.

This step is a critical part of the process since it assists you in transferring the information you are learning from your short-term memory into long-term memory; it is *technically* a phase you could skip if you only need the information for a short period of time. Still, even in such a circumstance, it is recommended that you follow this step like all others.

Review

Similarly to the previous step, you perform this one at the very end of the chapter—and then you must both recall your questions, as well as the eventual answers that you found for said queries. Just as listed in the prior section, if you fail to do so, then you may look at your textbook, but should also consider re-reading the chapter—or, at the very least, the section that was relevant to the answer(s) that you forgot.

Overall, following the various parts of SQ3R allows you to unlock the true potential of learning by reading—having the truly great benefit since reading-based study materials tend to be the most common.

Feynman Technique: Simplicity and Efficiency

For a breath of fresh air after the more in-depth tutorial of the detailed SQ3R technique, this section contains all you need to know about the intelligent system created by Richard Feynman. Something particularly notable about this four-step process is how simple it is; it is easy to explain and implement, making it quick to digest and remember.

The first step, Study, is that you choose what subject you are going to learn about. To add a bit more depth and detail, you can write down what you know about the topic, allowing you to break it down and granting you a greater overall understanding of it.

Afterward, the second step is Teach; as the name implies, you are going to teach the subject to someone else. Yes, that is correct—before you learn something, you are going to educate someone else on the subject! Now, you are free to pretend to teach someone by having someone imaginary rather than an actual person; however, it is recommended that you get an actual person if you are able to; they can highlight what you need to learn more about.

Thirdly, now that you properly understand where the holes in your knowledge are, it is your job to fill those in. Step 3, Fill the Gaps, has you studying the topic, *specifically* focusing on the areas that you were unable to teach during the second step. This is why step 2 was important—if you already know how 2 + 2 works with mathematics, then you should not need to study addition, and you can skip right over that section and jump right into multiplication.

And finally, as a certainly fitting capstone for this simple procedure, the last step is Simplify: Break down what you know into smaller, simpler parts, so that you can reference it later with ease. You can repeat step 2 with the simplified notes that you have, to see if it has properly helped you with understanding what you needed to know.

All of this makes up the Feynman Technique, a system that, while it is extraordinarily simple, can also be significantly effective.

Bloom's Taxonomy

Created by Benjamin Bloom with his colleagues, this section fits less into the "strategy with steps you can follow" category of smart systems but instead is a way to "rank" the differing levels of educational objectives. As a tool, it cannot be used on its own like many of the others listed here—instead, it should be used in tandem, to improve the overall effectiveness of your preferred study method. This section will list the rankings from the revised 2001 edition of the taxonomy, beginning with what would be at the very bottom of the rankings (and, thus, most important to handle first), before ending off with the very top of the "pyramid".

Remember

At the absolute bottom of the taxonomy is the most important aspect of education; without the ability to remember, you certainly will not be able to learn. For the best way to engage with this part of the structure, you can perform various tricks to enhance your memory—such as strategies involving "linking" your thoughts together, described in earlier chapters of this book.

Understand

The second rung is about understanding—in more specific terms, it could be summed up as the summarization and interpretation of the medium that you are working with. It can best be harnessed by looking at the topic through a more "overall" lens, doing your best to sum it up to prove that you have a general concept of the entirety of its scope.

Apply

Perhaps surprising in how it is not the last level, "apply" refers to the actual execution of the skills outlined in your education. In a sense, one should look at this part of the taxonomy with the idea that "doing is the best way to learn"—you cannot just read and watch; but instead, have to push onwards and grasp your knowledge with your own hands.

Analyze

After applying, it is important in the case of Bloom's Taxonomy to examine your work; organize it in a way so that you can analyze how every step was taken, see if there are ways in which it is similar to other skills that you have, and highlight their differences. On its own, this step may appear perhaps unfinished—but that is because it functions as groundwork for the level above it.

Evaluate

Through using the analysis created in the prior phase, this is the step that relates most to self-improvement. While the previous rung was more focused on laying the information out for you to work with, to evaluate properly is to receive critique—from yourself, or from others—and determine how best to proceed. Much like anything that requires a degree of creativity, you will need to experiment, listen to feedback, and be resilient in the face of challenges.

Create

Lastly, the highest level of the taxonomy is the idea of "creation"; in particular, this could be thought of more like the "future plans" phase of the system. After you have completed every other part of the pyramid, you are just before the end of the cycle of education— but now you have to create a plan for the next time that you engage with it. All of the information that you have absorbed up until this point becomes a proper tool for you here, allowing you to increase your efficiency in the future by scouting it out in the past.

Regardless of which of these systems you find is the most beneficial, or if you prefer a more "pick-and-choose" method making use of the strategies found earlier in this book, you should have the knowledge required to conquer almost any difficulties you will find when it comes to your chosen path of education.

Chapter 10:

Clever Tools You Can Use

At this point, after reading all that you have in this book, you should have a solid concept of the strategies that you will proceed with; if not, then you should take care to reread whichever chapters you found difficult in deciding on. However, for those of you who have a better grasp of what your plan is going forward, then this penultimate chapter (and the last with formal advice) will serve as the last stretch before the finish line—my last bits of knowledge to impart upon you, in hopes that it will make the overall learning process easier to parse with.

This chapter contains four tools for use with your learning—compatible with really any learning style, due to their general-use nature. If you find that you struggle with the *overall* parts of the learning process, I hope that the tools listed here will allow the learning process to be easier; if you do not have such issues, you may still find that using these recommendations makes the process all the simpler for you.

Flashcards: Avoiding Cramming, Enjoying Spacing

When it comes to wanting to learn faster, there is always going to be the temptation of cramming—just shoving all of the learning into a very short period, so that you can get on with your life as soon as possible. Unfortunately for those who want to save the maximum amount of time, it has been shown by numerous studies—such as the one by Kornell (2009)—that cramming rarely works—*some* knowledge may be kept, but for the most part, it tends to be a fruitless effort that increases stress, decreases focus, and is most certainly *not* a replacement for proper studying strategies.

Instead, you can try to use flashcards. Flashcards are indeed very simple, and they may remind you of public education to the point where you wonder if they even work—but they truly do! In fact, it has been found that the most efficient use of flashcards is through creating larger stacks of flashcards, each pile dedicated to an area in the topic at hand, and then spending a day combing over the cards—the actual size of the stack depending on the depth of knowledge required for the subject, but provided it is enough information to take up an entire study session, any amount should function well. On the other hand, you *could* create multiple, smaller stacks of flashcards, allowing you to look into more aspects of the subject in a single study session; however, doing so has the same flaws of cramming, limiting the amount of knowledge that you will actually be able to absorb.

What exactly you should write on the flashcards will depend entirely on the skills that you are trying to learn; it may be beneficial to have more exact terminology and concepts written down, or perhaps something more "loose" will suffice for your learning style. In the end, what matters the most is that you keep the cards within the general scope of a single "area" of knowledge within your subject and have them written in whichever style would be the most beneficial to your understanding—whatever that may be. As with all things found within this book, the degree to which subjects and preferences can vary means that experimentation will naturally be required for finding the method that works best for you.

Something that should be kept in mind with flashcards is the fact that their organization is just as important as what is actually *on* said cards; you could indeed keep all of them in a single binder or desk drawer but doing so risks mixing them. As stated above, it is best if you keep flashcards organized into stacks so that you can keep all of the cards of a single area of a topic together. Alternatively, it can be quite useful to have the cards in locations that are relevant to the subject at hand.

For instance, if you are using flashcards to study facts about gardening, then you could put one stack of cards in a location near where you keep your gardening tools (with this stack being based on those tools, of course), and another where you keep seed packets. By doing this, you create a logical location for them—much better than having them somewhere random to the point you might lose them, like how many people tend to lose their keys due to lacking a specific location for them. This also creates a connection in your mind; when you are working with those seeds, you will naturally tend to think about the flashcards you had placed near the seeds, and thus their information will be at the forefront of your mind—so, if you made sure that the knowledge contained was relevant, then it will enhance your experience significantly!

Pictograms: Visual Comprehension

Maybe flashcards, with their focus on words and reading, are not your preferred style? It is very common for people to struggle when it comes to information in a text format; of course, perhaps you could consider it ironic to state such a thing near the end of a primarily text-based work, but it is still worth stating, nonetheless. In a study on how pictograms use text-based labels compared to pictograms as warnings, it was found that it was about four times as likely for the picture-based warnings to be heeded and remembered in comparison to their text-only counterparts. As a result, it is clear to see that it is not uncommon to prefer images to text when it comes to information processing.

Implementing pictograms into your learning will vary in terms of a subject by an even greater level of magnitude than most other bits of learning advice—for a more visual medium such as painting, it will naturally be easier to create fitting pictograms. On the other hand, for a work that is more cerebral and abstract, such as storytelling, you may find it challenging to properly convey complicated topics into image formats; in such cases, one way you can allow it to fit better is by breaking it down into pieces. Rather than having a single pictogram represent the entirety of how to write the concept of the hero's journey, you can instead create a pictogram for each of the steps along the way; thus, when viewed as a *whole*, they represent the hero's journey, overall serving as a reminder of how to write in such a structure.

If you still have difficulty remembering what the contents of the pictogram refer to, then you might consider adding a label to the image; to some extent, you could argue it defeats the purpose of having the image at all, but the nuance captured by the picture can be supplemented through a one- or two-word explanation. This could be especially useful if the pictogram is of a more surreal concept, one that could not be conveyed succinctly with just an image; thus, by adding a label, you help bridge the gap between your present self and your future self.

Just as was mentioned regarding flashcards, it is also imperative that wherever you keep pictograms, you make sure the location is one that makes sense to you—you would not have a warning sign about deer crossing in a location with no deer, after all, would you? The same principle can apply to your personal, educational pictograms; their consistent location not only serves as an easy way to remember where they are, but it also becomes a reminder of the knowledge contained within if they are near other relevant parts. In a sense, you can almost think of the location itself as a secondary pictogram, doubling the amount of visual information, all with a clear goal: Assisting you in remembering the skills you have spent so much time learning.

Tricking Your Mind with Learning Games

When it comes to learning, one of the hardest hurdles to overcome is the issue many people have with engaging themselves; they can learn when they are *forced to*, but for something that is as intrinsically motivated as self-education, it can become a challenge to actually take steps beyond the first few. This is where learning games come in—by turning the educational process into something you find fun, there is a natural inclination towards being *significantly* more engaged; even a game that is somewhat mediocre can still be enough to give that "push" towards learning.

The specifics of what kind of learning game will work best will depend significantly on your medium; you will have to examine the topic in-depth and identify what sorts of challenges could be turned into something that you could derive entertainment from. If you are looking into writing music, then you could perhaps try and read a book or think about a fictional character, and then challenge yourself to turn the story of what you experienced into a simple song—because yes, even though it is a learning "game", it does not necessarily need to be one with points. All that matters is that there is a level of enjoyment to it and that it draws your interests; unlocking the part of your mind which focuses on your wants rather than your needs is the key to bridging that gap.

If you are fortunate enough to have peers you are learning with, then creating a learning game can be an excellent step forward making a cooperative experience with them, where you all work towards challenges together, and have some fun at the same time. You could easily create a point system based on the work being done, with your team trying to score a certain number of points within a timeframe. Alternatively, you could attempt to make a more competitive game to enjoy with them—though competition actually tends to harm learning more than help it, so it should only be done if you and your peers can play the game with a very "casual" mindset so that your emotions do not get the better of you.

Of course, it is worth noting that while learning games are very useful, you should not get carried away with them; game design can be exceptionally fun, but if you spend too long on it, then you may find that the game actually ends up *distracting* you from your education, rather than adding to it! The best way to do this is by stepping back and examining not just the learning game itself, but also the educational experience as a whole when you brought said entertainment into the mix; in fact, did you actually find it improved the efficiency of your information absorption? Or did it serve as more of a distraction, something to keep your mind busy so you *did not* pay attention to what was going on? If you find that the results are less than desirable, you may want to reconsider the approach you took toward learning games—either for the specific challenges that you were trying to use or potentially even for learning games as a whole!

Binaural Beats: Manipulating Your Brainwaves

It would not be unreasonable to assume that you have heard of the three suggested tricks listed above—they are relatively simple concepts, and so they have permeated education systems throughout the world, used by many students and teachers alike. Binaural beats, on the other hand, is a much more niche topic; it can be applied broadly to the learning style of many people, but it is not a style of studying that many people have heard about!

First off, to explain what they actually are: Binaural beats are a form of music that makes use of two different tones simultaneously, each with a different frequency, creating an illusion in the brain that assists your ability to focus and comprehend information. It has been found that using this sort of melody heightens one's ability to relax, decreases a person's anxiety levels, and increases positive tendencies—all of which are quite useful when it comes to something that can be as mentally taxing as self-education! It is not some sort of miracle musical "cure-all" that will solve all of your problems when it comes to education, but it *will* grant you superior focus to the point that you can process what is going on with your learning to a greater extent than before.

Another benefit to binaural beats is the fact that they are extremely easy to access—simply put, all you need is a device that can play music, and a pair of headphones (though for the latter, some claim that you can still reap the benefits *without* headphones). You will need to find some of these beats online, but they can be easily located on websites such as YouTube by just searching for "binaural beats"—and then all you have to do is begin to listen while you work. The Zen-like state that these tones put you in can be relaxing to the point that some might fall asleep to it—and there is certainly nothing wrong with using it to help you sleep, of course—but it is important that you remain awake and dedicated to your studying when using these beats.

To properly turn it into a schedule, it is recommended that you try a variety of beats you find, seeing which ones heighten the learning experience most for you; after that point, you can either create a playlist of your favorite beats or even just loop the same melody repeatedly to the point that it can become proper white noise. The important part is making sure that you do not get *so used* to it that you lose the benefits; it is best if it can "fade into the background" so that you can focus, but it is bad if it fades so much to the point that you might as well not even have them on. As with all things, you will need to exercise a level of restraint, and—of course—experiment around with what works best for you.

It should also be noted that the phenomena found in binaural beats can also be found in standard music, from time to time—usually more from genres such as psychedelic rock, jazz, or other kinds of songs that tend to a "smooth" flow, rather than that which is more "jagged", such as metal or rock. Despite that, however, individual music tastes and how you respond to songs, in general, are going to be the deciding factors in what genre—if any—you could use as a substitute or supplement to binaural beats. Typically, what works best for most people is to put on a single specific song that has a decent level of repetition, and just keep it on a loop; rather than having a playlist that cycles through a variety of different stimuli, using the same melody for multiple hours can put the mind into a sort of trance, where all it is focused on is the learning itself. It can even serve to make the specific song an audible reminder of what you learned—perhaps when you put on Pink Floyd, you might think about how to write a horror story. At the end of the day, the specifics will be based on your taste in music, and that is something that you, yourself, will know far better than anyone.

I sincerely hope that at least one of the tools listed here ends up making the learning experience more enjoyable for you, as well as allowing you to engage easier. The process of self-education can be a difficult one when you are just starting out, but when you find the right knowledge, it can become much easier. Like everything, it will take practice to get used to, provided you use information like that contained in this chapter, you will find that it will come naturally in time. All you have to do is keep at it, be willing to try new things, and find out what works best—to make sure that you are not just coasting along, but that you instead pick the right tools for the job, get into the proper mindset, and charge on forth with a proper plan of action in your mind.

Conclusion

N ow that you have reached this chapter, it means that this is the end of your first step on the path to accelerating your learning. I sincerely hope that the information contained in this book will be of great use to you—some of it can be subjective, not every bit of advice will apply to every single person, and there will certainly be challenges that could not feasibly be included in a book meant to be for all interested, motivated learners. However, rather than attempt such an impossible task, the intention of this book has been not just to grant specific advice on how to accelerate your learning with named techniques and styles, but also to provide the skills needed to handle those challenges on your own.

Of course, that does not mean that you should disregard this book; the advice contained inside is legitimate, and if you found any of it useful, then you will likely want to revisit it at a certain point. As I have promised with this piece, it is my every intention to assist you on your educational journey however I can—through the medium of this written work, at the very least. Thus, the best final resource

I can share with you is a summary of the chapters you have read, so that if you want to revisit specific pieces of information in the future, you can flip to this concluding chapter as a guide; though, of course, you are also free to re-read the entirety of the book as much as you like.

Chapters 1-3: Principles of Accelerated Learning

These first three chapters make up the book's explanation of what accelerated learning is, the benefits of making use of it, and how best to conceptualize it. Of the chapters in this book, they are arguably the most important, since they lay the groundwork for the rest of the work to take shape; certainly, they are useful to revisit if you need reminders about the nature of accelerated learning itself, and this section is actually the most recommended for you to return to once you have set this book down.

Perhaps you may have had some questions written down about this book itself, like many of the pieces of advice listed inside it recommended you do with other texts? If that is the case, then these three chapters are, of course, the most natural starting point for asking and answering such queries.

Chapters 4-6: Proper Process, Practice, and Procedures (Primarily)

These chapters, now that you have been informed on what exactly accelerated learning is, outline how to actually begin the process of using it—if the first three could be seen as a "what" and "why", then *these* three are more akin to a "how to". If you find that you struggle to actually proceed with self-education, then these are excellent chapters to revisit, for the advice contained inside tends to be the most generally effective; regardless of the learning strategies that you determined were the absolute best, the information in chapters 4 through 6 should be applicable.

This collection of chapters also contains a very critical piece of information, which I feel is relevant enough to repeat here just one last time: Experimentation is key. Self-education is a deeply personal process, and while it can be fun to read an educational book and assume that every single piece of advice will always work for everyone and that it just boils down to picking what sounds the fastest; in reality, that is rarely the case. Instead, you will have to try out many things, and the majority of them will fail—what matters most is that you are willing to take that failure and turn it into a pair of wings, the kind that will let you soar toward success.

Chapters 7-10: Customizing Your Education

And then lastly, in this third part of the book is what could best be described as "customization"; not every person learns in the same way, and so when writing this book, there was the inherent challenge of determining how to give information that was simultaneously broad, but yet could also assist with specific difficulties a person may face. When it came to it, the best approach soon came to light: Allow the reader to understand the intricacies of learning itself, so that they may pick and choose what will work best for them—much like a person's sense of fashion, it can be hard to pick out an exact, perfect outfit for a person that they will be happy with. However, you can at least teach the individual the fundamentals of fashion, and soon they will be able to wear clothes that they find pleasing and attractive.

These chapters are the ones I expect will be revisited the most, especially since I have continuously recommended experimentation; as a result, unless you are particularly fortunate or self-conscious when it comes to your learning style, you should expect these chapters to be the ones you come back to more than others. I hope more than anything that you find the techniques here to be useful for your practical experiences, as they have done so for me endlessly.

And, following up on that, I hope that these brief summaries will be useful for any future rereads you have; once more, feel free to read the entire book again if you so please, but do not feel obligated to do so. The most important step when it comes to any sort of learning is that you are able to feel engaged, and so if the best method for you to use this book is to just reference small bits and pieces of it, then I will not stop you. I can only hope that my advice has had the impact I expected and wish you the best of luck on your educational journey.

References

Accelerated Learning Principles. (2009). Learningdoorway.com. https://www.learning-doorway.com/accelerated-learning-principles.html#:~:text=Accelerated%20 Learning%20Principles%20derive%20from

Accelerated Learning. (n.d.). The Peak Performance Center. https://thepeakperfor-mancecenter.com/educational-learning/learning/theories/accelerated-learning/

Ahrens, F., Oelschner, H., & Ahrens, F. M. (2017). Damage on Roller Bearing Races and Gear Teeth – Classification and Methods of Analysis. *Practical Metallogra-phy*, 54(7), 469–484. https://doi.org/10.3139/147.110462

Alamargot, D., Terrier, P., & Cellier, J.-M. (2007). *Written Documents in the Workplace.* In Google Books. BRILL. https://books.google.com.ph/ books?hl=en&lr=&id=U6vzAgAAQBAJ&oi=fnd&pg=PA17&dq=picto-grams&ots=3gnftK8-17&sig=BGanpzTzpaprLuDB0M9omiDr9uM&redir_es-c=y#v=onepage&q=pictograms&f=false

Armstrong, P. (2010, June 10). *Bloom's Taxonomy.* Vanderbilt University. https://cft. vanderbilt.edu/guides-sub-pages/blooms-taxonomy/#:~:text=Familiarly%20 known%20as%20Bloom

Associative Learning: Definition, Theory & Examples Video. (2021). Study.com. https://study.com/academy/lesson/associative-learning-definition-theory-examples.html

Ausubel D. & Youssef M. (1965). The Effect of Spaced Repetition on Meaningful Retention. *The Journal of General Psychology*, 73:1, 147-150, DOI: 10.1080/00221309.1965.9711263

Bernardes, F. (2019, December 31.). *Accelerated Learning Techniques: 18 Tips for Super Learning.* Classpert.com classpert.com/blog/accelerated-learning-techniques

Brookfield, S. (2003). A Critical Theory Perspective on Accelerated Learning. *New Directions for Adult and Continuing Education*, 2003: 73 - 82. 10.1002/ace.90.

Burns, K. (n.d.). *Running head: Single-and Double-loop Learning.* https://kaburns.people.ua.edu/uploads/3/7/3/2/37324267/kburns_-_single-double-loop_learning_theoretical_synthesis.pdf

Fletcher-Wood, H. (2018, April 22). *Step by step: Breaking Learning down Using Behavioural Psychology.* Improving Teaching. https://improvingteaching.co.uk/2018/04/22/step-by-step-using-behavioural-psychology-to-break-tasks-down/

Haaparanta, L. (2005). The Analogy Theory of Thinking*. *Dialectica*, 46(2), 169–183. https://doi.org/10.1111/j.1746-8361.1992.tb00091.x

Huber, J. A. (2004). A Closer Look at SQ3R. *Reading Improvement. (41:2), 108.* https://www.proquest.com/openview/fec54fde2be8271521864443b5d-ccdf0/1?cbl=2030479&pq-origsite=gscholar&parentSessionId=ISdcyH-G8lZmcU1QbL6JNqqHcLVP6CVw76rAfMQa5Y1s%3D

Karpicke, J. D., and Henry L. R. (2008). The Critical Importance of Retrieval for Learning. *Science*, 319 (5865), 966–968, learninglab.psych.purdue.edu/downloads/2008_Karpicke_Roediger_Science.pdf, 10.1126/science.1152408.

Kornell, N. (2009). Optimising learning using flashcards: Spacing is more effective than cramming. *Applied Cognitive Psychology*, 23(9), 1297–1317. https://doi.org/10.1002/acp.1537

Marques, J. (2012). The Dynamics of Accelerated Learning. *Business Education & Accreditation.* 4 (1), 101-112.https://papers.ssrn.com/sol3/papers.cfm?abstract_id=2005248

Marx, K. (2022, February 28). *Step-By-Step Plan for Leaders to Support Teachers.* Learning Sciences International. https://www.learningsciences.com/blog/deliberate-practice-marzano/

Nichols, M. H., & Cator, K. (2008). *Challenge Based Learning.* [White Paper]. Cupertino, California: Apple, Inc. https://www.challengebasedlearning.org/wp-content/uploads/2019/03/CBL_Paper_2008.pdf

Northern Illinois University Center for Innovative Teaching and Learning. (2012). Experiential learning. In *Instructional guide for university faculty and teaching assistants.* https://www.niu.edu/citl/resources/guides/instructional-guide

Oregon State University. (2019, August 22). *Memory: It's a Process.* Oregon State University Academic Success Center. success.oregonstate.edu/learning/memory.

Rajan, A., Hashim, A., Akre, V., Walid, H., Nassiri, N., & Ahmed, M. (2018, November 1). The Impacts of Binaural Beats. 2018 Fifth HCT Information Technology Trends (ITT), 353-357. https://doi.org/10.1109/CTIT.2018.8649538

Reflective Teaching. (2017). Yale.edu. https://poorvucenter.yale.edu/ReflectiveTeaching

Sascha. (n.d.). *Introduction to the Zettelkasten Method.* Zettelkasten Method. https://zettelkasten.de/introduction/

Self-Explanation, Interleaved Practice, and Other Learning Techniques. (n.d.). Psychology. ucsd.edu. https://psychology.ucsd.edu/undergraduate-program/undergraduate-resources/academic-writing-resources/effective-studying/other-learning-techniques.html#:~:text=Interleaved%20practice%20%E2%80%93%20when%20you%20are

Short, J., & Hirsh, S. (2021). *How to Implement Accelerated Learning Successfully | Professional Learning for Educators.* Carnegie Corporation of New York. https://www.carnegie.org/our-work/article/how-implement-accelerated-learning-successfully/

Swenson, C. (2003), Accelerated and Traditional Formats: Using Learning as a Criterion for Quality. *New Directions for Adult and Continuing Education*, 2003: 83-92. https://doi.org/10.1002/ace.91

Taylor, K. and Rohrer, D. (2010). The Effects of Interleaved Practice. *Applied Cognitive. Psychology*, 24: 837-848. https://doi.org/10.1002/acp.1598

Usable Knowledge. (2017). *The Value of Listening*. Harvard Graduate School of Education. https://www.gse.harvard.edu/news/uk/17/09/value-listening

Wallis, C. (2017, November 22). *A Better Way to Study Through Self-Testing and Distributed Practice*. KQED. https://www.kqed.org/mindshift/49750/a-better-way-to-study-through-self-testing-and-distributed-practice

What Is Strategic Learning? (2019). Ball State University. https://www.bsu.edu/about/administrativeoffices/online-and-strategic-learning/about

Why Use Games to Teach? (2018, May 7). Starting Point. https://serc.carleton.edu/introgeo/games/whygames.html